CLASSROOM MANAGEMENT
& BEHAVIORAL OBJECTIVES

L

To positive and creative teachers, as exemplified by *Karen Helmle,* originator of many ideas contained herein

Contents

Preface

Classroom Management and Behavioral Objectives brings together the areas of learning theory and classroom applications of that theory. Although it is impossible to provide the answer to every classroom behavior problem, a single, well-proven theory—learning theory—does apply to every such problem. If a teacher can relate the problems and objectives of a given classroom to this common theory, discussed in Part I, the development of effective and efficient programs will be greatly facilitated. Concrete examples of application, selected from my experience, are included throughout the text. To further illustrate the relationship between theory and application, a series of studies performed by teachers in their own classrooms has been included in Part II. The studies sample a wide variety of chronological ages and behavioral problems.

Additional applications of theory can be found in a companion book, *Materials for Classroom Management: Catch 'Em Being Good*, which provides samples of materials that the teacher might find useful in management programs. (Those materials most likely to be useful in the classroom are presented on worksheets for duplicating masters to simplify reproduction.)

Classroom Management and Behavioral Objectives and its companion manual, *Materials for Classroom Management*, will be of great interest to anyone concerned with teacher performance—teacher trainees, supervisors, administrators, and, of course, teachers themselves. Because of the emphasis in the books on practical application, they will also be relevant to in-service training and courses in curriculum and instruction, special education, educational supervision, and educational and school psychology.

TERRENCE PIPER

Philadelphia

PART I
Approaches to Good Teaching

Introduction

The ideas associated with such terms as behavior modification, classroom management, and learning theory are simply part of good teaching—and teachers have been using these concepts for years while emphasizing terms like consistency, precision, positive approach, and good planning. The new versions of these good teaching approaches are explored here and applied to classroom strategies.

The concepts we are concerned with are derived from learning theory. A learning theorist might be typified as an experimental psychologist who insists on scientifically pure experimental designs. Until recently, people generally were considered too complicated to be used as subjects in pure behavioral research, because they possess unwanted variables in their behavior, environments, and learning histories. Therefore, the classical learning theorist has used rats and pigeons as subjects in experiments. Current research, including the work of B. F. Skinner and many who followed him, has demonstrated that the principles of behavioral change (with some exceptions) can be generalized to apply to people as well as to any organism capable of learning. The basic learning principles remain constant throughout the animal kingdom. We will see how these principles apply to man—in spite of the exceptions that must be made because of the nature of human intellect, especially man's ability to speak. Let's look at the application of these principles in social and academic classroom learning behavior.

Behavior

Science is empirical and, therefore, deals only with what is observable. Learning theory has scientific origins, and efforts to study learning rely on behavioral observations. Human learning is conceptualized in behavioral terms, because learning cannot be observed and behavior can be. *Behavior, then, is any activity that can be observed.*

When behaviors are described precisely, it is possible to count the occurrences of those behaviors over a period of time and to indicate the extent of time during which they occurred. Both possibilities are quantifiable, and precise descriptions of them can be made.

COMMUNICATION: A CASE FOR BEHAVIORAL DEFINITIONS

Classroom activities are described as exactly as possible, so that they can be counted and so that the descriptions convey the same meaning to everyone. For example, to say "Today Jack studied hard" can mean so many different things to different people that the statement is nearly meaningless. The most consistent meaning conveyed by such a statement is probably that the teacher was not irritated with Jack—but that tells us something about the teacher, not Jack. Let us examine a more behavioral statement: "During independent seatwork periods (9:30–10:00, 11:00–11:30, and 1:30–2:15) I observed Jack in his seat, eyes directed at his paper or book, and pencil in hand. He left his seat on three occasions, once to sharpen his pencil and twice to go to the library. He finished his arithmetic worksheets and reading workbook tasks with 90 percent accuracy and reported making progress on his weekly social studies project." This description is longer and demands more effort on the part of the teacher, but because it is meaningful and useful, it wastes fewer words than the short and obscure first statement. Notice also that the second description is student centered rather than teacher centered. In fact, we know less about how the teacher feels from the second statement than from the first one. What most of us are asking for when we say "be specific" is a description of behaviors rather than a description of how someone feels about or interprets the behaviors. To make the point clearer, let us look at another example.

Report cards (with or without grades) are great sources for teachers' comments that are too general to be meaningful. Statements such as "tends to be hyperactive, is a sensitive child, has poor peer relationships, is making progress" mean little to a parent, or worse—mislead a parent, unless the parent has a behavioral list of what such terms mean to the teacher. What, exactly, does *hyperactive* mean to Miss Smith? Let us examine the statement, "Willie is making progress." To a parent, or anyone else, the statement will likely mean that in Miss Smith's opinion there is no reason to worry about Willie's school work. But again, the statement is more teacher centered than child centered. The parent still has no description of what Willie is doing or can do. Consider how much more would be communicated if Miss Smith had sent all parents lists of sight words and/or phonetic skills to be mastered by the children in reading throughout the year—arithmetic skills presented in hierarchies and spelling words to be mastered, for example. Then, instead of saying "Willie is making progress," Miss Smith might be able to make such statements as: "Willie has added the following words to his sight vocabulary . . . , and he has progressed from skill 4 to skill 7 in his addition skills." If Miss Smith were totally sold on a behavioristic approach, she might also include samples of the tasks that Willie performs in proving to the parent that he has acquired certain skills. Imagine how impressed the parent would be to be told what his child can do! You may argue that such communication requires too much work and time. However, if the teacher is planning as extensively as she should be, and if she is taking a diagnostic approach, she is probably already keeping such records. Why not share them with parents?

OBSERVING BEHAVIOR

Counting. Thinking behaviorally is not difficult after the habit is developed. Think of a child you have known whom you might label "hyperactive," or "rebellious," and describe his behavior. Now ask yourself, could you *count* the child's activities in your description? Could you present your description to another teacher so that he would count the same behaviors that you do? Could you make accurate comparisons between days, or weeks, by comparing the results of your counting?

You may be wondering whether the amount of counting that is required interferes with teaching. The answer is to simplify the counting procedure by counting a particular behavior for only a sample of school time, 15 or 30 minutes, for example. It is also expedient to count students' written responses because they can be tallied after school hours if necessary. Teachers aides or students can assist in the counting.

To make evaluations of your programming as a teacher and of the child's progress as a student, you must count in order to make comparisons. For instance, there is no better way to decide which of two reading books is more effective than to use both and count appropriate behaviors with each. Unless a teacher's observations are behaviorally oriented, and unless he counts behaviors during these observations, he must live and work in a world of uncomfortably subjective guesses. To rephrase that, the teacher must be a sort of behavioral scientist. He must make comparisons between materials, techniques, and children if he is to be able to guide the right child in the right way at the right time, and if he is to be able to make evaluations of his techniques. The teacher who, instead, relies on feelings and "plays it by ear," is doing a disservice to himself and his students.

Attitudes as behavior. You may feel that you cannot think in behavioral terms about everything and that many important areas such as attitudes and self-concepts are not behaviors. True enough. In fact, learning itself is not truly a behavior since it goes on inside the child's head, where we cannot measure. And yet, such a statement serves to support behavioral thinking, because *the only way we know anything about anyone is through observations of behavior* or through reports of observations made by others. Therefore, if someone suggests that Miss Smith has certain bigoted attitudes toward minority members and that these attitudes interfere with her teaching, it is because someone has made observations of Miss Smith's behavior. The behavior may have been verbal and expressed in the teacher's lounge or it may have been gestures and verbalizations by Miss Smith within the classroom. It is true that some behaviors are so subtle, such as certain voice inflections or facial gestures, that we have great difficulty in speaking of them, much less measuring them. But they are behaviors nevertheless, so that we may still regard such a complex social phenomenon as racial prejudice as a behavior. Except for believers in ESP, there is no other way to know another person than by observing behavior.

The advantage of behavioral description is that it provides an accurate picture of performance. If Miss Smith's principal is aware of a growing consensus that she is a racial bigot, and there are many children from various minority groups enrolled at his school, he would have cause for concern. As a good administrator, he would be less concerned with a general term like "bigot" than with what Miss Smith is *doing* that has caused the term to be applied to her. Consciously or not, the principal has become a behaviorist, as most of us do when very important decisions are to be made. He observes Miss Smith and notices that she seldom calls on minority children, but he also notes that the minority children seldom raise their hands. Miss Smith has grouped the children for reading and nearly all the children in the slowest group are minority children. Segregation? He's not sure, because these children do seem to be the slowest readers. He notes that Miss Smith's eye contact, smile, and verbal praise are more often directed at white students. Finally, in conversation with Miss Smith, he realizes she refers to "them" when referring to minority children and "our" when refering to white children. (Note that calling on students, hand raising, grouping, eye contact, smiling, verbal praise, and pronoun usages are all behaviors, and could be counted.) The principal now has firsthand observations rather than hearsay remarks about Miss Smith's behavior, and he can use his observations in confronting Miss Smith with her classroom partiality and in helping her change some of her behaviors.

BEHAVIOR MANAGEMENT AND BEHAVIORAL OBJECTIVES

The behavioral approach described thus far should not be isolated from other developments in education. Current concerns for better evaluation and student-centered planning have given rise to an emphasis on *behavioral objectives.* Quality classroom management requires setting up behavioral objectives and being behaviorally objective as well. But classroom management principles carry the usefulness of behavioral objectives one step further than planning and evaluation. Application of these principles can determine how frequently the particular behavior will occur. The frequency of appropriate versus inappropriate behavior will determine how well a classroom functions and how much progress the children can make within that classroom. Classrooms in which appropriate behaviors, as defined by the teacher, occur at very high frequencies are well managed. Hence the term *classroom management principles* is most appropriate. Classroom management principles are most directly concerned with what happens immediately *after* a behavioral objective has been met or has not been met by a particular child. Since what comes after the objective has been met is important, time is important.

REVIEW QUESTIONS

(Answers to Review Questions begin on page 127.)

1. Because learning goes on inside our nervous systems, we can most easily measure learning by observing changes in _____.
2. Before scientific approaches to learning are possible, we must _____ behavior.
3. Behavioral definitions or objectives may seem long, but they _____ fewer words.
4. The process of counting behaviors is made easy by
   (a) Counting during only a part of the day, such as 30 minutes
   (b) Counting written responses
   (c) Using aides, including the children themselves
   (d) All of the above
5. The only way we know anything about anyone's mind is through _____.
6. Applying the principles of classroom management can determine _____.

CHAPTER 2

Antecedents and Consequences

TIME

Every behavior occurs in time. While this fact may seem obvious and elementary, it is significant that behaviors occur in a measurable time span. In addition to the time element, every behavior is preceded by some stimulus and every behavior is followed by some stimulus. Let us refer to the stimuli that precede a particular behavior as that behavior's *antecedents*. The stimuli that follow a particular behavior will be referred to as that behavior's *consequences*.

Antecedent(s)	Behavior	Consequence(s)
Time		

As an example, let us imagine a child named Jimmy has raised his hand in class. The behavior here is Jimmy raising his hand. The antecedent stimulus may have originated with the teacher. She may have said "Who has the answer to question 7?" or "Who would like to pass out the paint brushes?" The antecedent might also have come from Jimmy's peers. Perhaps Billy has just ripped up Jimmy's paper, or Jimmy has just noticed Mary copying his work. The antecedent may also have come from outside the classroom—Jimmy might have seen the first robin of spring through the window. Lastly, the antecedent may have come from Jimmy's work (e.g., if he could not solve an arithmetic problem) or from a physical need (if he needed to go to the lavatory). These last two possibilities are unique in that they involve minimal prompting from Jimmy's surroundings; consequently, these antecedents are not behavioral. Antecedents cannot always be behaviorally defined.

The consequences of Jimmy's behavior, raising his hand, are easier to anticipate than the antecedent possibilities, because the consequences will all entail some sort of teacher attention. Usually, the teacher will have eye contact with Jimmy and may even make a response such as "Yes, Jimmy?" Or, she might move toward his desk. Let us ignore all the antecedent possibilities, save one, in order to be more specific: Teacher asks, "Who knows the answer to question 7?" (antecedent). Jimmy raises his hand (behavior). Teacher has eye contact with Jimmy and says, "Yes, Jimmy?" (consequence). What could be simpler than A, B, C—antecedent, behavior, and consequence; this sequence represents the simplest unit of behavior much as the molecule is the simplest unit of an element. However, just as a molecule of gold may not be very representative of the whole item such as a gold wedding band, so too the simplest unit of behavior may not be very representative of a larger whole such as a lengthy and complex series of verbal interactions between two individuals. In the example of Jimmy and his teacher, the antecedent and consequence both come from the teacher and are closely related to each other. Note that if we were concerned with the teacher rather than with Jimmy, the antecedent and consequence would represent two *behaviors* on the part of the teacher. In the two teacher behaviors, Jimmy's raised hand becomes a consequence for the teacher's first behavior (asking question) and an antecedent for the teacher's second behavior (calling on Jimmy).

Teacher: *(teacher's question)* Behavior #1
Jimmy: *(teacher's question)* Antecedent

Jimmy: *(hand raise)* Behavior #2
Teacher: *(Jimmy's hand raising)* Consequence for behavior #1
(Jimmy's hand raising) Antecedent for behavior #3

Jimmy: *(receives teacher attention)* Consequence for behavior #2
(receives teacher attention) Antecedent for behavior #4
Teacher: *(teacher attention)* Behavior #3

Jimmy: *(answers question)* Behavior #4
Teacher: *(Jimmy's answer)* Consequence for behavior #3
(Jimmy's answer) Antecedent for behavior #5

In the interaction between the two individuals, the behavior of one individual (Jimmy's hand raising) serves as both a consequence for what has gone before (teacher's question) and an antecedent for what is to come after (teacher's next behavior).

THE BASIC OPERANT PRINCIPLES

How cues become cues. We might say that antecedents are cues, or as the psychologists would say, discriminative stimuli, that indicate when a particular behavior is appropriate or inappropriate. Almost any behavior you can imagine is appropriate in certain situations (the situation contains the cues or antecedents) and is inappropriate in others. A child may learn that to raise his hand when he has a question is appropriate in his classroom, but inappropriate when eating dinner with his family. As adults we know that certain garments in our wardrobes are appropriate in some situations and inappropriate in others. We have learned what is appropriate or inappropriate for certain situations, and we have done so through experiences with consequences. For this reason, *consequences cannot be separated from antecedents.*

Johnny discovers that raising his hand in his classroom generally leads to an answer to his question. Since an answer to his question is what he wanted, it may be considered a *positive consequence.* When a consequence for a certain behavior is positive, then that behavior is *appropriate* for that situation. Since raising his hand worked in school, Johnny might raise his hand to ask a question when his family is assembled for dinner. Instead of an answer, the consequence to his behavior here is laughter, which is not what he wanted, so he perceives the consequence as negative. When a consequence for a certain behavior is negative, then that behavior is *inappropriate* for that situation.

Similarly, Miss Schmit finds that wearing her green dress brings frowns from her peers, and snickers from her students when she wears it to school. Yet when she wears it to a party, she is complimented and gets a great deal of male attention. Miss Schmit has learned that her green dress and others like it are appropriate for parties, but are inappropriate for school. She has learned through consequences. Antecedents develop their discriminative value (hence the term *discrimination stimuli*) between appropriate and inappropriate situations through consequences.

The four kinds of consequences.   There are only four basic kinds of consequences possible for any behavior: (1) a reward is introduced, (2) a punishment is introduced, (3) a reward is removed, or (4) a punishment is removed. Notice that there was no room left for a fifth alternative that might be called "nothing was introduced or removed," but remember that "nothing happening" after we do something is really not nothing happening. We all do what we do in order to gain something (type 1) or to get away from something (type 4). Therefore, "nothing happening" is either an example of consequence 4, punishment removed or delayed, or of consequence 3, reward removed. That is, the reward

that the behavior was intended to produce did not materialize so that the reward was, in effect, removed, or the punishment that the behavior was intended to avoid did not materialize, so that punishment was, in effect, removed. (See Table 1.)

To suggest that we do what we do in order to gain or avoid something may be a disturbing thought. Isn't one too "self-centered" and "shallow" if all his behavior is directed at gaining rewards or avoiding punishment? No. We do what we do for reasons. To do something without a reason would be less than psychotic (even psychotics have reasons); it would be vegetative, random behavior. Note that the reasons for behavior relate directly to gaining rewards or avoiding punishments. One may make value judgments about the rewards being sought or punishments being avoided, but there is no value judgment to be made about the presence of a reason. Note that the terms *reward* and *punishment* are not limited to monetary or material gains and losses. Social approval and disapproval, power, knowledge, and even religious experiences may be involved.

Now let us examine the additions to the behavioral sequence in Table 1. Just as discriminative stimulus is the technical term for cue, there are technical terms for the consequences. Introducing a reward as a consequence is called *positive reinforcement* and introducing a punishment as a consequence is called *punishment*. Removing a reward as a consequence may be called by one of two terms, depending on how it is done. If a reward that has been presented after a particular behavior is simply omitted and the behavior is otherwise ignored, the change in consequence is called *extinction*. If a child is removed from a rewarding situation so that he cannot receive rewards, the procedure is called *time out*, an abbreviation for "time out from positive reinforcement."

TABLE 1

Time		
Antecedent	Behavior	Possible Consequence
Cue	Defined so that it can be counted	1. Introduce reward
		2. Introduce punishment
		3. Remove reward
		4. Remove punishment

TABLE 2

Time

→

Antecedent	Behavior	Consequence
Discriminative stimulus	Defined so that it can be counted	1. Positive reinforcement 2. Punishment 3. Extinction and time out 4. Negative reinforcement

The difference between extinction and time out might be summarized as the difference between ignoring behavior and removing the child or the reward from a rewarding situation. Removing a punishment as a consequence is called *negative reinforcement*, an unfortunate term which can be easily confused with punishment. Yet, of course, it is certainly not punishment. (Even experts of long standing make errors using this confusing terminology.) We can now add the technical terminology to our table (see Table 2).

Examples of the four types of consequences are everywhere—every behavior's consequence falls into one of the four categories. Let us consider the effect of each consequence on behavior by examining some common examples of each of them.

EFFECTS OF CONSEQUENCES

The effect of positive reinforcement. Remembering that positive reinforcement is the introduction of a reward after a behavior, what would you expect to happen to a behavior that is followed by positive reinforcement? Would the behavior increase in frequency in the future, or would it decrease? (Check one.)

_____*Increase*   _____*Decrease*

Johnny sees Billy get a sucker (antecedent), Johnny cries (behavior), teacher gives Johnny a sucker (positive reinforcement for Johnny). In layman's terms, Johnny's crying worked. It paid off. So in similar situations in the future, Johnny is going to use what works (you might say we're all pragmatists). His crying will increase.

If you checked "increase," you're with me. If you checked "decrease," ask yourself why. Think of some examples in your own life and remember that positive reinforcement refers to rewards that are really rewarding to the person doing the behaving. There is only one way to know that something is "really rewarding," and that is by observing the effect

of the consequence on the behavior. If Johnny's getting a sucker caused him to cry less in the future, then we would know that there is something about the sucker or the way it was delivered that Johnny dislikes. If the sucker is truly a positive reinforcer, it *must* cause the behavior to increase. Therefore, the increase in the behavior that is followed by the sucker is evidence that suckers are, to Johnny, rewards that can be used in positive reinforcement. (Keep in mind that the occurrence of an increase or decrease in a behavior pinpoints much of why we must count behaviors.)

The effect of punishment. Remembering that punishment is the introduction of an aversive stimulus after a behavior, what would you expect to happen to a behavior that is followed by punishment? Would the behavior increase in frequency in the future or would it decrease? (Check one.)

_____ *Increase* _____ *Decrease*

Johnny sees Billy get a sucker (antecedent), Johnny cries (behavior), Teacher says "I've had enough of this," and spanks Johnny's bottom (consequence). Again in layman's terms, and assuming that what

Johnny really wanted was a sucker, we might say that Johnny's tactic did not work. In fact, it was a disaster. He will be less likely to try crying next time he sees teacher give Billy a sucker. So, you should have checked "decrease."

But what if the crying increased? Then the spanking episode must be, for Johnny, a reward. He might be said to crave the intense attention he receives from the teacher when he's spanked. We have no way of knowing exactly why he behaves in order to maximize his opportunity to get spanked. But we do know that being spanked, under the given circumstances, is *positive reinforcement* for Johnny if his crying continues. If the teacher is counting behaviors, this unusual aspect of Johnny's personality will become clear and she will change her mode of punishment.

It should be stressed that this example concerns Johnny's crying after he sees Billy get a sucker, not his crying behavior after the teacher spanks him. This would be a second and very different behavior probably designed by Johnny to be a punisher (consequence) for the *teacher's* behavior (spanking) if he wanted that particular teacher-behavior to decrease in the future.

The effect of extinction. Remembering that extinction is the withholding of positive reinforcement after a behavior in a situation where the behavior was formerly reinforced, what would you expect to happen to a behavior that is followed by extinction? Would the behavior increase in frequency in the future, or would it decrease? (Check one.)

                ____*Increase*   ____*Decrease*

Johnny is a "spoiled" child. For many years, his parents have made sure that Johnny got whatever he wanted when he cried or whined. But teacher behaves differently from Mommy and Daddy. On the first day of school, Johnny sees teacher give Billy a sucker (antecedent), Johnny cries (behavior), teacher continues working with other children, ignoring Johnny except for instructing other children to do the same (consequence). We will assume that Johnny cried in order to create a consequence (receipt of sucker) as he had learned from his parents. Now, with the teacher, crying seems to do no good. In effect, the anticipated reward has been removed. Put yourself in Johnny's shoes. What would your behavior be?

This time either increase *or* decrease might be correct. On a short term basis, Johnny's crying might increase in duration and intensity. We might imagine him saying to himself "hmm, this crying routine isn't working this time; I must not be doing it good enough. Maybe if I try a little harder and make it a bit more traumatic . . . ." But the long term effect on the crying, if it really doesn't produce any rewards for Johnny, will surely be a reduction in crying when working with the teacher. Crying doesn't work anymore, so why cry. It's no fun in itself. Note that if the behavior was "fun in itself," that is, self-rewarding, extinction would not work.

The effect of time out. Remembering that time out is the removal of a reward from the child, or the child from a reward (rather than an anticipated reward as in extinction), what would you expect to happen to a behavior that is followed by time out? Would the behavior increase in frequency in the future, or would it decrease? (Check one.)
_____*Increase* _____*Decrease*

Once again, Johnny sees the teacher give Billy a sucker (antecedent). The children have been playing a word game and Billy's sucker means that he is the winner. The children have come to expect the game to be played three times in a row before going on to another activity. All the children look forward to playing the game. Immediately after the antecedent, Johnny cries (behavior). Teacher explains to Johnny that he cannot play the next game, but should go back to his seat and calm down. If he can compose himself before the beginning of the third game, he will be allowed to rejoin the group. Here too we see that the crying behavior did not pay off. In fact, it resulted in a *temporary* loss. Therefore, we would expect the crying behavior to decrease. If it increased after the antecedent described, it would indicate that Johnny, unlike the other children, does not enjoy the game and is crying in order to *avoid* additional games. Notice that the time out procedure is "double edged" in that it incorporates reinforcement for the termination of the disruptive behavior. Johnny will be reinforced for stopping his crying by being allowed to rejoin the group.

The effect of negative reinforcement. Remembering that negative reinforcement is the removal of punishment after a behavior, would you expect a behavior to increase in frequency in the future or to decrease? (Check one.) _____*Increase* _____*Decrease*

Johnny sees Billy get a sucker (antecedent). Before that, Johnny had been disruptive and had interfered with the game the children were playing. The teacher told Johnny that he couldn't play anymore, and took away the sucker that Johnny had won in the preceding game. Now, after seeing Billy win and get a sucker, Johnny starts to cry (behavior). The teacher consoles Johnny by telling him that he can play again and by returning his sucker.

We might say that in this situation Johnny's crying behavior worked. The punishment that he received earlier has been removed as a consequence for crying. We can expect Johnny to cry more, given a similar set of cues in the future. His behavior is negatively reinforced. Notice that both positive reinforcement and negative reinforcement refer to consequences that reinforce (or strengthen) preceding behaviors. Positive reinforcement occurs in introducing rewards; negative reinforcement occurs in removing punishments. The effect is the same.

Consequences have effects in accordance with the principles of behavior change. The manager or teacher does not manage by changing or structuring the principles. The principles are laws not subject to change. Rather the manager structures contingencies. *A contingency is the if-then relationship between a behavior and its consequence.* For example, a teacher may say, "If you get 93 percent of the items correct, you will receive a grade of *A*." Receiving an *A* is contingent on producing a 93 percent correct paper. The teacher may praise contingent upon satisfactory assignment completion, or teacher attention may be contingent upon hand raising. There are many contingencies in any classroom.

REVIEW QUESTIONS

1. Significant stimuli that precede a behavior are called _____; those that follow are called _____.
2. The antecedents and the consequences for a particular behavior are principally defined by _____.
3. Significant antecedents might also be called _____.
4. Though antecendents cue behaviors (i.e. "now is the time to do this because of the cues I perceive), antecedents develop their cue value because of experience with _____.
5. We all do what we do in order to _____ or to _____.
6. Introducing a reward as a consequence is called _____.
7. Removing a punishment as a consequence is called _____.
8. A reward is a reward if it causes the behavior that precedes it to _____.
9. Punishment is really punishment only if it causes the behavior that precedes it to _____.

CHAPTER 3

Rewards That Are Rewards

As we have said, consequences can be thought of as either introducing and removing rewards or as introducing and removing punishments (i.e., aversive stimuli). What we have not said is what makes a reward a reward or what makes a punishment a punishment.

Most teachers assume that they know what is rewarding to their students, and usually such assumptions are correct. Yet, when an error is made, how does the teacher discover the error? For example, Mr. Brown wants Jerry to sit in his seat more often. If Jerry leaves his seat, Mr. Brown frequently provides a verbal consequence such as "Jerry, sit down." As the day goes on and as weeks go by, Jerry continues to get out of his seat too often. Mr. Brown's voice becomes more and more stern. Mr. Brown knows that this tone of voice has been effective for many children. Since Mr. Brown's stern tone of voice is introduced as a consequence to a behavior in order to decrease the frequency of that behavior, Mr. Brown is attempting to use his stern voice as punishment. Yet Jerry's out-of-seat behavior seems to be occurring at greater and greater frequencies. It is certainly not decreasing.

BEHAVIORAL REACTIONS TO CONSEQUENCES

Based on the four fundamental behavioral consequences, we can suggest two possibilities for Jerry's behavior. First, Mr. Brown may be correct in his assumption about the punishing quality of his voice, but there may be rewards for the student's behavior that are outweighing the punishment provided. In other words, Jerry may be, in some way, so rewarded for his out-of-seat behavior that the relatively mild punishment provided by Mr. Brown is not effective.

The second, and more likely, possible explanation is that Mr. Brown is incorrect in his assumption about the punishing quality of his voice as far as Jerry is concerned. Perhaps Mr. Brown is the first male teacher Jerry has ever had, and to add drama, perhaps Jerry lives alone with his divorced mother. Jerry craves Mr. Brown's attention, and his stern-voiced attention is probably the most intense attention Jerry can get. Therefore, Jerry gets out of his seat because doing so is followed by intense attention from Mr. Brown.

Of the two possible explanations, Mr. Brown can quite easily decide which is correct. He can count the number of times Jerry leaves his seat for several days; *then he can systematically ignore the behavior, never giving Jerry any attention when he's out of his seat.* (Of course, Mr. Brown would attend to Jerry as before when he is in his seat.) If the first explanation is correct, Jerry's reaction to being ignored when he's out of his seat should either be no change or that behavior should become more frequent. If the second explanation is correct, Jerry's behavior should begin to improve: he should be in his seat more frequently.

REWARD AND PUNISHMENT DEFINED

If it should turn out that the second explanation is verified, Mr. Brown has been in error about the aversiveness of his stern voice. When the stern voice follows Jerry's behavior, the behavior increases. Therefore the stern voice is not punishment. It is instead a reward.

Stimuli that follow a behavior, and that result in an increase in the frequency of that behavior are rewards.

Surely you have known children who enjoy making certain adults angry. Those adults undoubtedly assume that their angry behaviors are punishing. But for the child to whom they are amusing, the angry behaviors may be rewards. Therefore, the children will continue to do whatever they do that makes certain adults angry. Errors in assumptions about rewards and punishments are not as uncommon as one might imagine. You will never make such an error for long if you observe what happens to the behavior preceding the consequence.

In the example with Mr. Brown and Jerry, we have seen a reward used when it was assumed to be punishment. Let us imagine a situation in which punishment is used when the manager assumes that the consequence is rewarding.

Mrs. Berg is a speech therapist. She sees Jimmy twice a week to work on his articulation errors. Jimmy often replaces the *r* sound with a *w* sound. Mrs. Berg shows Jimmy pictures and asks him to tell her stories about the pictures. She has records that indicate that the error occurs on

94 percent of initial *r*'s, 76 percent of the medial *r*'s, and only 14 percent of the final *r*'s. For treatment, Mrs. Berg pops an M&M into Jimmy's mouth whenever his *r* is accurate, To her surprise Jimmy fails to improve. In fact he is slightly worse and seems to be avoiding words with *r* sounds in his stories. A stimulus (M&M) is introduced after each correct behavior and there is a decrease in the frequency of the behavior. The M&M, either the taste or the way and circumstance under which it is presented, is an aversive stimulus. It is punishment.

Stimuli that follow a behavior and result in a decrease in the frequency of that behavior are aversive stimuli or punishers.

A more common example of an individual who attempts to reward, but in reality punishes, is the "social gusher." A "social gusher" is one of those extremely complimentary persons who compliments you on such things as your appearance, personality, wit, voice, and taste, regardless of how you look and so forth. The gusher is probably rewarding (or rather attempting to reward) you for spending time with him. Yet, if the gusher were to count the seconds you spend with him, he would see that the tallies are decreasing in magnitude. Since his compliments are resulting in a decrease in your behavior, that is, the time you spend with him, his compliments are punishing.

Take a moment to test yourself on the two definitions we have just covered. Remember, a reward is any stimulus that, when introduced after a behavior, results in an increase in that behavior. An aversive stimulus as used in punishment is any stimulus that, when introduced after a behavior, results in a decrease in that behavior. Assume that the variables mentioned in the test items are responsible for the behavioral changes.

1. Mom praises baby every time baby goes potty on the toilet. Baby goes potty more on the toilet more often. The mother's praise is

    _____.

2. John asks Mary about her health after Mary greets him in the morning. Mary greets John in the morning less and less. The inquiry about Mary's health is _____.

3. Johnny has temper tantrums whenever teacher keeps him in for recess. The tantrums include screaming and breaking objects in the room. Teacher keeps Johnny in less and less. The behavior is the teacher telling Johnny he cannot go out. For this behavior Johnny provides _____.

4. George's parents tell him it is time to go to bed. George begins to cry. The parents allow George to stay up for one more TV program, if he stops crying. George cries, when first told to go to bed, more and more often. What his parents do after he begins to cry seems to be _____.

5. Jim discovers that by marking things in his store at very high prices and then putting them on sale at what he had originally intended to sell them for, his sales go up. Soon Jim is having more and more sales. Jim's sale behavior has been _____.

KEY: 1. Rewarding   2. Punishing   3. Punishment
4. Rewarding   5. Rewarded

CLASSROOM REWARDS

Elementary school. Now that we have discussed how erroneous assumptions can be detected, it may be helpful to list assumed rewards that can be used in the classroom. Adapt this list to your own elementary school classroom by omitting the rewards that are impossible within your limitations and adding as many possibilities as you can imagine.

List of assumed rewards

Foods and drinks

Carrot and celery sticks	Olives and pickles
Cereal	Popcorn
Fruit (fresh and dried)	Nuts
Fruit juice	Soda
Milk	Sweets

Social (given with enthusiasm and sincerity)

Verbal

"Good"	"Superb"
"Very nice"	"Sterling"
"Outstanding"	"Terrific"

Nonverbal

Smiles	Pat on back
Hugs	Handshake
Kisses	

Symbolic

Grades	Written praise
Stars	Points
Smiling-face sticker	

Graphing
   Line graphs with frequency plotted across time
   Bar graph
   Posters with child's name where stars, stickers and points can be
      accumulated
   Picture graphs where child earns apples for the tree, eggs for the
      basket, etc.

Classroom "jobs"
   Water plants   Errand runner
   Erase blackboards   Book distributor
   Dust   Paper collector
   Milk monitor

Classroom privilege
   Leader in line   Paper corrector
   Direct singing, or select song Open surprise package
   Select story to be read   (provided by teacher)
   Leader in game such as
      "Simon Says"

High-interest activities
   Field trip (earned by class)   Work in interest corners:
   Class party (earned by class)   art, science, library,
   Free time to work on projects   animals, and plants
   Play with games in the room   Read a library book
   Help another student

Honors
   Good grades
   Certificates of achievement
   Diplomas
   Completed contracts

Communications
   Letter of praise to parents
   Phone call to parents regarding good behavior

Secondary school. The secondary school classroom offers especially
difficult problems in presenting a list of rewards. Adolescents are far
more sophisticated and will expect sophisticated rewards. Social reinforcement is simultaneously simple and sophisticated. Most adolescents
will be reinforced by approval from a teacher capable of establishing

himself as someone to be respected—someone who knows his subject matter, is up-to-date with what juveniles know, and works to prepare well-organized, concise, and relevant classes.

Adolescents need peer approval as well, and teachers can organize the curriculum to provide for such approval. For example, a social studies teacher might present a lesson with a problem-solving format. By grouping students into teams and allowing team members to interact as much as they like, students with more knowledge about a problem will receive both attention and praise from fellow team members.

Two math teachers might cooperate so that once a week their classes compete in the "High School Math Bowl." Students might earn points on classwork, homework, and tests that are exchangeable for a position on the team representing their class.

Grades, though often misused, can be very effective reinforcers. If a teacher gives weekly grades and lists exactly what the student must do to earn each grade, students who have made no progress at all may suddenly begin to work diligently. For example: The teacher may say that from Monday to Friday, the students who earn 100–115 points will receive an *A*, 90–99 points a *B*, 80–89 points a *C*, 60–79 points a *D*, and 0–59 points an *F*. Students can earn as much as 20 points each on two homework assignments (40 points total). They can earn up to 10 points for discussion on each of the three class days devoted to discussion (30 points total). They can earn up to 20 points for class work on the day set aside for research (20 points total), and they can earn as many as 25 points on the weekly test. Therefore the "perfect" student can earn as much as 115 points. The teacher must be objective in awarding points and quick to inform the student when points have been earned.

Time to work on special projects can also be an effective reward at the secondary level. The projects may be individual, group, or class, but time to work on the project must be earned by satisfactorily completing the more mundane aspects of the curriculum. Needless to say, the projects must be of special interest to the students.

REVIEW QUESTIONS

1. A reward, by definition is _____.
2. We can correct erroneous assumptions about what is rewarding by simply _____.
3. List at least five potential rewards in your classroom not mentioned in Chapter 3.

4

Positive Reinforcement Superior to Negative Reinforcement

As soon as a teaching contract is signed, a teacher accepts responsibility for the behavior in the classroom. In doing so, the teacher will attempt to decrease undesirable or irresponsible student behavior and to increase desirable or responsible behavior. In order to bring about desirable student behavior, teachers basically rely on either positive reinforcement or negative reinforcement. If the teacher chooses negative reinforcement as the effective consequence, it will mean that the students must be caught being bad in order for the teacher to act appropriately. If positive reinforcement is chosen, the teacher must concentrate on catching the students being good. Most teachers undoubtedly do some of both, but tend to use either one consequence or the other more frequently.

POSITIVE REINFORCEMENT PREFERRED

We can cite five reasons for preferring positive reinforcement to negative reinforcement. The first reason might be called the *humanitarian reason*. It is simply more pleasant, kind, and humane to spend the teaching day rewarding children than punishing them. Not only will the teachers be happier, the children will surely be happier as well.

The second reason might be called *sociological*. The classroom managed with rewards will have an atmosphere of freedom, while the classroom that relies on negative reinforcement and punishment will seem oppressive and dictatorial. If the contingency for doing some work is a promise of reward, the child may choose to do the work with the feeling that he still has a choice. (Of course, he does not have a choice if he wants the reward.) The reward acts as an incentive. But when the child is threatened with punishment, the choice seems to be gone. (Of course, it is still there if he is willing to accept the punishment.) The threat of punishment acts to inhibit. To give an example on your own plane of experience, suppose your boss is moving and offers to pay you $100 if you will help. You assume that your boss will not be angry if you refuse, so you feel free to help or not help. Yet you will probably help, if at all possible, in order to gain $100. On the other hand, your boss could say that you must help him move or he will deduct $100 from your paycheck. How free would you feel in this situation?

The third reason to rely on reward or positive reinforcement is that in administering punishment the teacher is far more likely to make an *error*. That is, it is quite possible that the child will be rewarded rather than punished in the teacher's attempt to punish. For many good reasons, teachers are forbidden to use harsh forms of punishment, and only the rather mild reprimand and removal of privilege remain as legal forms of classroom punishment. Coupled with this problem is one that is unavoidable: punishment involves very intense attention giving. Consequently, teachers who have students that crave attention may inadvertently increase undesirable behavior in attempting to decrease it.

The fourth reason is based upon the same *basic operant principles* we have already discussed. All of us respond to our environment in an effort to control it; if you punish a child, he will want to return that treatment. Suppose you have just punished a student by removing his recess. Will he want your recess-removing behavior to increase or decrease? Obviously, he will want it to decrease, and he has the same alternatives to use to decrease behavior that you have—punishment, time out, and extinction. Children can punish teachers in many ways, for example, by not doing work, crying, and pouting. The child who suddenly acts as though the teacher doesn't exist is using extinction. No teacher wants her students to punish her or even to want to punish her.

The fifth and final reason to prefer positive reinforcement requires an explanation of Pavlovian conditioning. In the early 1900's Pavlov clarified a process involved in conditioning called *respondent conditioning*.

Pavlov and the conditioned response. In respondent conditioning one must begin with an already well-established stimulus-response link. That is, a stimulus such as a sudden loud noise is followed by a response such as a startle reaction. Furthermore, in respondent conditioning the response is one that people do not ordinarily control at will. Once the stimulus is perceived, the response follows automatically. The response can be traced to glandular or other chemical changes in the body over which we have no control. Such behaviors as heartbeat, sweating, and pupil dilation are examples. The response used in Pavlov's classical experiment was salivation. Once the stimulus and response are identified, respondent conditioning proceeds by pairing the stimulus with a second stimulus. Remember that the response automatically follows the first stimulus. After many presentations of the two stimuli together, the response will eventually be elicited by the second stimulus *in the absence of the first stimulus.* A new stimulus-response link has been learned, and constitutes the respondent conditioning.

In Pavlov's classical experiment, dogs were the subjects. The stimulus-response pair that was already known by the dogs was meat powder→ salivation. Since the stimulus-response sequence was not taught to the dogs, Pavlov claimed that the sequence was unlearned or unconditioned. Pavlov labeled the meat powder the *unconditioned stimulus* (UCS) and the salivations the *unconditioned response* (UCR). He chose the sound of a bell as the stimulus to be paired with the meat powder. The sounding of a bell is not ordinarily followed by salivation in dogs. The bell was paired over and over again with the meat powder. After many trials the dogs salivated when they heard the bell, even if there was no meat powder. Inasmuch as this bell-salivation sequence was learned, Pavlov called the bell the *conditioned, or learned, stimulus* (CS) and the salivation to the bell the *conditioned response* (CR). Figure 1 shows a diagram of the process. Notice that the UCR and CR are essentially the same behavior.

You may be wondering how research with salivating dogs in Russia can ever be applied to your classroom. Actually, the same principle is applied almost constantly. All respondent behaviors are due to glandular or chemical changes within the body. Our emotions and our likes and dislikes are respondent behaviors. Even Pavlov's dogs' apparently

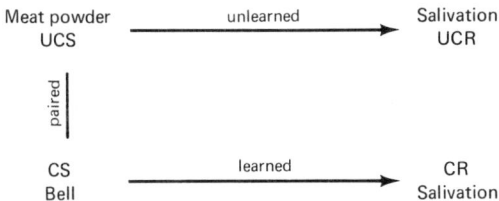

FIGURE 1.   A diagram of the derivation (in Pavlov's theory) of the conditioned response.

unimportant behavior of salivation is no longer unimportant when we realize that we are likely to salivate a great deal when experiencing a positive emotion or good feelings, and very little when we experience a negative emotion or bad feelings. Salivation is one of the few scientifically empirical ways to measure the degree to which someone feels positive affect.

Up to this point we have talked about how rewards and punishment affect behavior, how to identify rewards and punishments, and what rewards might be available. But we have not yet explained how rewards become rewards in the first place, nor how aversive stimuli become aversive. Pavlov's apparently simplistic research becomes most important and relevant when we realize that he discovered how rewards become rewards.

THE NATURE OF REWARDS

Primary rewards. There are rewards that are unlearned, that are "built-in," and though these rewards may vary from species to species, un-learned rewards are those that are necessary to sustain life. Food, drink, air, sleep, sex, and the opportunity to eliminate waste are all necessary for man and most animals. These are called *primary rewards* or *unconditioned rewards*, for they are not only unlearned but also the first rewards from which other rewards are generated.

A primary reward is a pleasurable unconditioned stimulus with an unconditioned response.

Research efforts more recent than Pavlov's suggest that man may have primary rewards in addition to those required to maintain the body and species. Harry Harlow's work at the University of Wisconsin in Madison in the late 1950's suggested that there may be primary rewards that are tactual; monkeys being raised without mothers preferred a cloth-covered dummy mother to a very similar surrogate of wire without cloth covering.* The preference was maintained especially when the baby monkey was startled or confronted with an object he feared, even when a filled baby bottle was placed in the wire mother's body. Harlow's research suggested that human infants may be experiencing primary, unlearned rewards when being held and cuddled by the mother or a mother substitute. In fact, reports of sickness and death among infants raised in certain sterile, "unloving" foundling homes of several decades

*Harry Harlow, "The Nature of Love," *American Psychologist*, 1958, *13*:673–685.

ago further suggest that infants may require such touch for physical health.

Another primary reward may be stimulation of almost any kind. A series of studies referred to as *sensory deprivation studies* investigated the effects of nonstimulating environment.* Subjects, usually college students, were paid to relax for as long as they could in stimulus-free environments. They were placed in sound-proofed rooms, given no light, and encased in clothing and cushions so that they received very little tactual or kinesthetic stimulation. Within a few hours, the subjects found their situation intolerable. Many exhibited psychotic symptoms until they returned to a normal environment. In the extreme, at least, stimulation of any kind may be a primary reward.

In more normal circumstances the need for stimulation may produce curiosity, and answers or other stimulations that satisfy curiosity may to some extent be primary rewards. While more research is still to be done in this area, the concept can be applied to the exploratory behavior of the toddler. Perhaps the two-year-old child is reinforced for emptying mother's dresser drawers by simply finding out what is there.

Learned rewards—the conditioned response. Although some rewards are unlearned, the great differences between cultures and subcultures clearly indicate that most of the rewards we work for, at least their particular varieties, are learned. Even individuals of the same sex, age, and subculture may not like or dislike the same people or things. We differ in what we like because each of us has a different learning history, though those histories may all be based on the same set of primary rewards.

Let us assume that for baby John, milk is a primary reward, an unconditioned stimulus that is followed by the unconditioned response of feeling good (see Figure 2). Now, what stimulus is likely to be paired

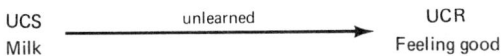

UCS	unlearned	UCR
Milk		Feeling good

FIGURE 2. An unconditioned response follows an unconditioned stimulus.

with the UCS, that is, what might be the CS? Most likely, the sight, sound, smell, and touch of someone who may later be called "mother." We all know that babies learn to love their mothers, or someone who

*For an example of these studies, see W. Heron, "The Pathology of Boredom," *Scientific American*, Jan. 1957.

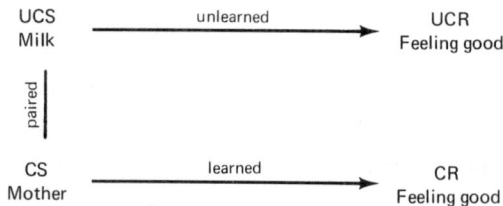

FIGURE 3. The unconditioned stimulus is paired with a conditioned stimulus.

substitutes for mother, because that person is paired with already rewarding stimuli such as milk and cuddling (see Figure 3).

Research that has followed Pavlov's classic experiment has further suggested that a CS–CR pair, once it is very well established, can function like a UCS–UCR pair. Let us assume that a mother, who is a conditioned stimulus (CS) for good feelings, has a favorite color which happens to be blue and frequently dresses in that color. If her daughter repeatedly pairs her with the color blue, the daughter may develop a special feeling toward the color blue, so that years later blue will be the daughter's favorite color.

To give another example, Jim loves the country, especially wooded areas. Jim grew up in the city. Whenever his father could afford a vacation, he would take his family to a wooded part of the state where the father and his son would camp and fish and do all sorts of things that Jim enjoyed. Because the woods were paired over and over with pleasant things that Jim enjoyed (father, vacation, fishing, and camping), Jim has come to love the woods. In fact, he commutes over forty miles to work in order to have a two-acre wooded lot.

All of us have learned to like things as a result of respondent conditioning—we all have favorite colors, hobbies, subjects, places, and people. Children, by the time they reach school age, have developed a complete set of rewards that you can incorporate into the management of your classroom. (Unless your teaching circumstance is bizarre, you will also want the children to like their school, their schoolwork, and their teacher.) Most rewards used in classrooms are learned rather than unlearned, and we know that learned stimuli (CS) for good feelings (CR) that are well learned can be used like unlearned stimuli (UCS). A complete diagram using intermediate CS's as though they were UCS's is shown in Figure 4.

UCS   UCR
(e.g., milk) $\longrightarrow$ (good feelings)

CS_1 CR
(e.g., mother) $\longrightarrow$ (good feelings)

CS_2 CR
(e.g., blue) $\longrightarrow$ (good feelings)

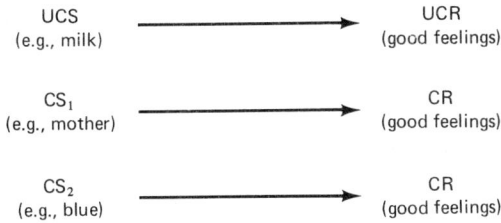

FIGURE 4. Conditioned stimuli can function like unconditioned stimuli.

CLASSROOM APPLICATIONS

Positive CS. A teacher begins the school year with children who have already learned many rewards to which they respond consistently. Assuming that these rewards are well learned, we shall treat them all as though they were built into the children's mental makeup, that is, as UCS's for good feelings.

Suppose a teacher decides to rely as much as possible on introducing rewards for appropriate behavior and on ignoring inappropriate behavior. That is, *extensive* and appropriate use of positive reinforcement and extinction is planned. The teacher praises good work, good answers, good in-seat behavior, good cooperation, and problem solving. The teacher ignores children out-of-seat, sleeping, and day-dreaming, goofing off, and giving wrong answers, and he returns sloppy or inadequate assignments without comment. He responds quickly and definitively to children who ask directions or seek guidance. Children who are making progress are given rewards of privileges, honors, or whatever is "extra special." The classroom has as few negatives as possible and a multitude of positives.

Consider the praise or any of the other rewards the teacher used, as a UCS for good feelings (UCR). What do you suppose will be paired with all these UCS's? What else will the children experience at approximately the same time as they experience the UCS? What will become the CS for good feelings? It should be apparent from the discussion on unconditioned and conditioned stimuli that if praise is a UCS for the children, then the person who is the source of that praise in the classroom will be paired with it, as well as the place where it occurred and particular activities that resulted in praise. The CS's in the example are

1. The teacher and people like the teacher
2. The curriculum and activities related to the curriculum
3. The classroom and places similar to the classroom

Beyond making good use of the conditioned stimulus, classroom management is easier for the teacher who is well liked and respected. Such teachers find their approval responses become greatly rewarding to the student and their disapproval responses quite effective punishment. However, being well liked and respected do not necessarily go hand in hand—people who are consistent and act appropriately (even if negatively) are respected; people who reward consistently and appropriately are liked and respected. Classroom management is further enhanced when the curriculum and the class is enjoyed by the children, and in this situation the curriculum can become self-reinforcing (e.g., the reward of reading a truly enjoyable book).

Negative CS.   In contrast, let us see what happens in the classroom where punishment is favored. We have all encountered the individual who waits for us to make a mistake in order to reprimand or insult, and never says a word when we perform well. Unfortunately, too many teachers react to their students' behavior in this way. Nearly all teachers are guilty, at times, of using negative approaches when they could easily be using positive ones; for example, it is a common classroom procedure to mark incorrect answers wrong and make no mark whatsoever after correct answers.

The Pavlovian model can be diagramed using punishment as the unconditioned stimulus rather than reward (Figure 5). The manager who punishes more frequently than he rewards will inevitably become a CS for bad feelings. However, a manager who frequently punishes and punishes appropriately and consistently will be respected. When punishment is used inconsistently, fear rather than respect results, because the child cannot find any formula that will allow him to consistently avoid punishment.

A Latin teacher who maintained beautiful control and had the respect

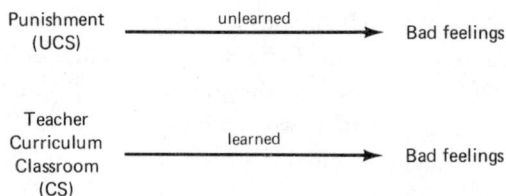

FIGURE 5.   Punishment substituted for reward as the UCS in the Pavlovian model.

of all her students was highly skilled at insulting and belittling her high-school students but would never do so unless the student seemed to be unprepared. Praise was never heard; her consistency eliminated fear because there was no uncertainty on the part of the students. However, she was honestly disliked by even her best students, and Latin became so unpopular that it was nearly dropped from the curriculum (an example of student use of extinction as a consequence in response to punishment).

Examples of negative CS can be more pathetic at the elementary school level. A veteran second-grade teacher had survived the pressures of inner-city teaching for nearly two decades. The principal had assigned her a room at the end of a dead-end hallway for good reason: she could be heard screaming directions, laced with insults, at any hour. She carried a ruler whenever she was in the presence of children, and slapping sounds could be heard from the hallway. Her room was a sort of well-guarded secret in the school, and as a visitor I had no opportunity to collect data on her students' behavior. But their expressions as they marched through the halls made it clear that no one could be doing more to create the chronic truant of the future than this teacher. The principal was no less guilty—he frequently praised her for her fine control. It seemed the only measure of success there was having a quiet class, no matter how.

Another teacher's view of negative stimuli can be seen in this next example—a more positive climax to Pavlov's implications. Miss Brown, a young, white teacher starting her first year of teaching had thirty third-grade students who were Black. After several weeks of class chaos, she was sure they were "out to get her" and was prepared to resign. With some encouragement from the principal, she agreed to accept the help of outside observers who watched her teaching the class for a week. Within the first few minutes of observation, it was apparent that the teacher was wrong about the students' feelings. The children *liked* her and they sought her attention constantly. She never used punishment, and the most negative consequence she offered was a serious person to person conference with a student about why children cannot do this or that in school. As you might guess, the kids loved it. She was not punishing them when she thought she was, and she was rewarding them at all the wrong times. For example, one of her class rules was to "raise your hand when you wanted help." But without knowing it, Miss Brown never helped a child with raised hand while we had the opportunity to observe. Even so, hand-raising was not completely extinguished, and many children still raised their hands—but only for a moment or two. Then, as though realizing they had made a mistake, they dropped them.

Put yourself in the child's place. You want help. What do you do? You might call out the teacher's name. That worked but it was not the most effective means because other children could intercept Miss Brown before she responded to your call. How could you be sure of getting her attention? Go to her, right? And if several other kids had the same idea? Pull on her sleeve or skirt. That was the most effective way, and more and more children were doing just that. If there were too many others already crowded around and pulling? Start a fight. Miss Brown's room was a circus in full swing. Yet because she was basically positive in her approach to the children, the problem was minor and easily remedied. No respondent conditioning had turned the children off to Miss Brown or school. In-service training showed Miss Brown how to be positive *at the right time*, and an immediate change occured in class-room behavior.

REVIEW QUESTIONS

1. List and briefly explain the five reasons for preferring positive management (positive reinforcement for good behavior and extinction for undesirable behavior) over negative management (punishment for undesirable behavior and negative reinforcement for good behavior).

2. Pavlovian conditioning can be summarized as follows: we learn to like things or events that are paired with _____ and to dislike things or events that are paired with _____.

CHAPTER 5

Generalization and Discrimination

To this point, we have established that everyone has built-in rewards and an array of learned rewards as well as built-in aversive stimuli and an array of learned aversive stimuli. Everyone does what he does for a reason: to maximize his rewards and to minimize the aversive stimuli. Cues, or antecedents, indicate when a behavior will be rewarded and when no reward will follow. Other cues indicate the same for punishment. Yet we know that all of us, adults or children, are confronted with constellations of cues that we have never experienced before. How is it that a man decides what to do to maximize his rewards when driving down a street that he has never driven down before, when entering a restaurant he has never entered before, when confronting a customer he has never met before, or when confronted with a lesson he has never experienced before?

THE BALANCE BETWEEN GENERALIZATION
AND DISCRIMINATION

If we were to learn to perform behavior X only when confronted with certain very specific cues, we would say that we are not *generalizing* our learning to any other cues. Suppose Jimmy learns to say "apple" when Miss Jones presents a card with *Apple* printed in black letters during reading time in his first-grade classroom. If Jimmy does not generalize to any degree, he will not know what to do when Miss Jones changes the color of the lettering, or changes from a card to a page in a book, or presents the card during recess on the playground, or when the card is presented in just the same way by a different teacher. Surely no one would have learned to read, or speak, or count, or do any complex task if they had not been able to generalize from one set of stimuli to other similar sets of stimuli. Yet we have all witnessed learning problems that are related to too little generalization. Any experienced teacher has been frustrated when a spelling rule is applied to one word and not another, or when a scientific principle is applied to one circumstance and not another.

The process opposing generalization is discrimination. The more generalization, the less discrimination; the less generalization, the more discrimination. We have suggested that without generalization we would have much less learning since everything would have to be relearned whenever a cue changed—and cues are constantly changing. In an opposite way but just as effectively, no ability to discriminate would end all intelligent activity.

Mother teaches baby to say "Hi," and baby says "Hi" but does not discriminate the occasion for saying it. Chance alone would seem to govern when baby says "Hi." Teacher teaches John that the answer to 2 + 2 is 4. But John does not discriminate between teacher's questions. He is as likely to answer "4" as anything else he's learned whenever asked a question. Even this example implies that John discriminates between teacher and others. If he does not discriminate at all, he may well answer "4" when mother asks him how everything was at school today.

Intelligent behavior requires a balance of generalization and discrimination. It is that balance that can explain how an individual is able to make rational decisions about what to do in situations that are simultaneously unique and similar to other situations that were experienced in the past. Each of us weighs the similarities of the antecedents and relative values of the consequences before reacting to new sets of cues. At the same time, we have learning histories with respect to generalization and discrimination. The individual who is considered to be creative and who can adapt his behavior to new circumstances readily and without hesitation has been heavily reinforced for generalizing, even from seemingly unrelated situations. The individual who is considered to be narrow-minded, inflexible, and conforming has been reinforced for discriminating and avoiding situations that demand extensive generalization. Remember that we can be reinforced positively by introducing rewards and negatively by removing or delaying aversive stimuli.

IMPLICATIONS FOR TEACHING

The implication is that teachers can do a great deal to reinforce creativity and to promote adaptability. However, to reinforce any and all generalization would be a serious error. We have seen how too much of either generalization or discrimination impairs learning. A second, and less important implication, is that it is true that people often behave very appropriately in situations that they never before encountered. Yet it cannot be said that their behavior was not learned nor that it wasn't learned through the contingency principles that we described.

In teaching creativity, the teacher can reinforce unusual or even bizarre answers that might have any small amount of plausibility. For example, if you ask a child where milk comes from, and the child says from llamas or even elephants, accept the answer with interest and enthusiasm. Then explain that both llamas and elephants produce milk for their babies that is very much like the milk in the cartons. You can point out that in some distant countries people do drink llama milk and make cheese from it, too; but you just don't happen to know much about elephant milk. When you eventually talk about cows as a source of milk, avoid the implication that the child's first answer was wrong or even foolish—because such a reaction would be punishing a creative behavior.

In addition, the teacher can structure certain situations such as science experiments or social problem solving that are not solved or figured out with the most obvious answers. The children will be challenged to think creatively in order to get closer to the answer, and that's the time to reinforce them. The standard science experiment with the hard-boiled egg and the milk bottle can be a delightfully stimulating problem for children. You present the class with a milk bottle that has the peeled egg whole and inside the bottle. Then you present several peeled eggs and several milk bottles to the students and offer them the chance to do what you did. The obvious solution will result in wrecked eggs. Only the very creative child will think of heating the bottle, placing the egg on top, and then cooling the bottle. In the meantime, you're likely to hear or see other interesting but unworkable solutions tried. Reinforce these solutions as well. The only caution here is not to reinforce a "solution" that has absolutely no plausibility.

REVIEW QUESTIONS

1. In school, a child learns to raise his hand when he has a question. At his first cub scout meeting, he raises his hand to ask a question. This apparently unlearned response is actually an example of _____.

2. The same child does not raise his hand when he has a question for mother at home. Not raising his hand when at home is an example of _____.

3. All complex intelligent behavior requires a blend of _____ and _____ .

4. A person who generalizes easily, but not to such an extent that he fails to recognize which responses are foolish, can be said to _____ very well.

5. If one generalizes well, one must of necessity also _____ well.

CHAPTER 6

Shaping and Fading

People learn new behaviors. Sometimes such learning can be attributed to generalizations from other learning. Yet generalizations alone cannot explain all new learning. For example, we do not learn to read by generalizing from math. Two other processes are involved—one we call shaping, the other fading.

SHAPING

Shaping deals with the criteria for reinforcement and relies on a bell-shaped curve for explanation. Let us suppose that you wished to teach a child to draw the letter A, and you plan to develop this new behavior using shaping only. You begin by giving the child the direction,

"Draw the letter A. It looks like this."

and present the letter model. If the child is quite young and has only rudimentary fine motor skills, he will produce a wide variety of responses to your directions such as

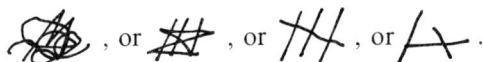

 , or , or , or .

You can see that some of the responses more closely approximate drawing A than others. In the example, the last attempt is closest to A and the second attempt is furthest from A. We can assume that A-drawing is a continuum between random marks made by the child and perfect A reproduction. At any point in time, a child's response when told to draw an A will cluster around some point on the continuum to approximate a normal curve. The curve of A-drawing will move up the continuum as the child improves his A-drawing ability. Figure 6 represents the A-drawing continuum.

FIGURE 6.   The A-drawing continuum.

For example, you begin with Johnny and get a good idea of where he is on the continuum by watching him to see what he does when you give the direction to draw an *A* (see the curve in Figure 7). To shape the behavior represented by the shaded area in Figure 7, you will reinforce responses that fall in the right-hand position of the curve. So while you ignore the first scribble as a poor response, you reinforce 𝓗𝓗 as a pretty good response. Imagine that you reinforce those behaviors in the shaded area of Figure 7. Johnny's curve of A-drawing will move so that it centers about the shaded area, that is, eventually his behavior will approximate the dashed line and move up the continuum. As he improves, the teacher should raise the criterion for reinforcement (Figure 8).

The manipulation of the criteria for reinforcement in order to alter the distribution of a given response to the right or left is the essence of the shaping process.

As the child improves again the criteria is increased again, until eventually the child is able to draw *A* so well that the teacher accepts the behavior without further improvement (Figure 9). A teacher improves a student's behavior by reinforcing only the better examples of the

FIGURE 7.   An example of a curve in beginning A-drawing.

FIGURE 8.   As A-drawing improves, the criterion for reinforcement is raised, and the curve advances along the continuum.

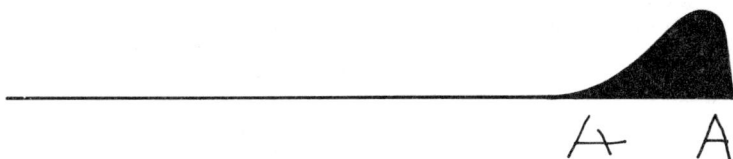

FIGURE 9.   The final curve for A-drawing.

behavior, and by demanding more for reinforcement as the child improves.

Teachers do this all the time without giving the process any thought. The first time a child says "da-da" he will surely be reinforced. As time goes on and he says "da-da" easily and sometimes says "daddy," the parents will eventually change the criteria for reinforcement from "da-da" to da-dy." A child growing up without such adult reaction will learn to speak very slowly, if at all. "When I first heard my daughter play a tune on the piano, I praised her for her rather awkward performance. Now that she has been playing for many years, I certainly wouldn't reinforce the same performance. I might even punish it." Sounds like another parent who used shaping without having so much as heard of the process.

Although in real-world applications of shaping and fading the two are generally used simultaneously, they are two completely separate processes. Shaping involves manipulations of the criteria for reinforcement and is in the consequence section of the antecedent-behavior-consequence chain. Fading, on the other hand, is a manipulation of antecedents.

FADING

Fading may be defined as the gradual elimination of antecedent cues so that eventually only one cue remains.

For example, you wish to teach a child to eat with a spoon. Before you begin, the child grabs his food by the fistful and shoves it into his mouth. If you put food on the spoon and rest the spoon on his plate, he takes the food from the spoon with his hand. Then he shoves it into his mouth. If you were to use shaping alone, you would have to observe his behavior to find out which of his behaviors was best, and then reinforce the superior behaviors. The process might be especially long and tedious, partly because in eating, every behavior that results in food in the mouth is reinforcing. Fading is likely to be more effective for this particular behavior.

First you find a spoon with a handle that is especially easy for the child to hold. Second, you see to it that the food the child is to eat is easy to eat with a spoon. (Mashed potatoes are easiest of all, but soft Jello can be impossible.) Now you are ready to begin the fading process.

Start with enough cues so that the child cannot fail. In the example, the child would require so many cues that the teacher would, in effect, go through the motions with him. Stand behind the child and grasp his hand around the spoon. Scoop up some food and raise it to the child's mouth. When he opens his mouth, tip the spoon and its contents into his mouth. Lower the child's hand holding the spoon to his plate until the food is chewed and swallowed. Then repeat the whole process.

As the child begins to know what to expect, you may begin to eliminate pressure cues. You needn't hold his hand so tightly. You needn't push or pull so hard. You gradually loosen your touch and gradually provide less guidance. Many meals later you merely touch the child's arm, and later still you are merely in the same room as the child when he eats. You have eliminated the cues that were initially necessary for the child to succeed. From the beginning, the child has been prepared to follow the cues since you allowed him to put food in his mouth in no other way, even if that means holding his other hand as well.

Teachers use fading whenever they provide supportive help, then remove the help as the student improves. Programmed texts often use fading to teach penmanship. Initially all the child is asked to do is trace an already existing letter. Then the letter is faded so that the child is connecting dashed lines. Eventually he produces parts, then whole letters with no cues other than the directions at the top of the page.

The teacher who helps the child in his oral reading, but helps him less and less as he learns more and more word attack skills is also using fading.

COMBINING THE TWO

As already mentioned, fading is seldom found without shaping and shaping is seldom found without fading. A natural teacher shapes and fades with little consideration for the complex sequences that she is following. Together, the processes explain how behavior modification techniques apply to behaviors that the child has not yet mastered. Since most classroom behaviors that teachers might call academic behaviors involve adding new behaviors to the child's repertoire, shaping and fading are of vast importance to any teacher.

REVIEW QUESTIONS

1. In order to teach a child new material, a teacher is likely to use both _____ and _____. Notice that both processes begin with what the child can already do and lead him to the new mastery.

2. _____ is a manipulation of the antecedents. So many helping cues are initially provided that the child cannot fail. Gradually, the cues are _____.

3. _____ is a manipulation of the consequences. All initial behaviors are accepted, but only the best are _____.

4. Therefore, less sophisticated responses are no longer reinforced. We might say they will decrease because of _____ procedures.

CHAPTER **7**

Social Considerations in Positive Management

Any good administrator will be quick to acknowledge the difference between being a good teacher and having a quiet classroom. Yet being a good teacher becomes impossible without some substantial degree of classroom control. We might say that a good manager is not necessarily a good teacher, but in order to get the chance to effectively teach, a teacher must be a good manager. As a good manager, the teacher must control children's social behaviors such as shouting, hitting, running, laughing, talking, and using foul language. The children have already mastered such behaviors and can perform them at will. No shaping or fading are required, and the application of behavioral principles remains relatively simple.

If you, as a teacher, pointed out the classroom behavior that you found most irritating, it would surely be social behavior. The kind of student behavior that makes it difficult for you to concentrate on your lesson is invariably social behavior. Let's see how the basic principles of classroom management can be applied to achieve control in the following steps.

PREPARING A MANAGEMENT PLAN

1. List all behaviors exhibited by children in your class that you wish were reduced or eliminated.

2. Now see if you can reduce the length of the list by finding items that, if controlled, would eliminate other items. For example, you may be able to eliminate "hitting" if it is impossible for one child to hit another when out-of-seat behavior is eliminated. Condense your list so that there are as few negative rules as possible. Remember, every item must be listed behaviorally, so that the behavior can be reliably counted. Be specific.

3. Put yourself in a positive frame of mind. Consider all the behaviors that you *want* your children to perform, and list those behaviors. This list is far more important than the first one, because by concentrating on this positive list you will have a valuable tool to use to eliminate behaviors on the negative list. Review the positive list item by item. When you find an item on the positive list which if increased would *automatically* require a reduction of some item on the negative list, note the negative item next to its respective deterrent on your list of positives. You will then have identified pairs of behaviors which are incompatible and, therefore, cancel each other out. For example, you may have included "unnecessary out-of-seat" behavior on your negative list and "in-seat studying during seatwork time" on your positive list. Clearly, the child who is in his seat and studying cannot be out of his seat at the same time. Consequently, an increase in in-seat studying behavior will inevitably be followed by a decrease in out-of-seat behavior. You may begin to imagine how your positive list, if inclusive enough, may make the entire negative list seem rather unnecessary.

4. List the rewards that could be used in positive reinforcement in your classroom. Material rewards are only a small part. Include in the list yourself, your personality, curriculum, privileges, high-interest activities, and evaluation. Use your imagination, and make the rewards list as complete as possible. List rewards for the individual student and for the class as a group.

Now you have established all the basic building blocks with which to create a management program. You know which behaviors you do and do not want, which of these compliment each other, and what contingencies (rewards) are available. Notice that, while you were asked to list rewards, no mention was made of lists of aversive stimuli that may be used in punishment. We have already established the desirability of a positive approach in managing behavior. A top-notch program, then, will rely on positive reinforcement (using the rewards) for the positive list of behaviors and extinction for the negative list. In classroom management, punishment will only be called for if (a) the behavior in question is dangerous to other children or jeopardizes school equipment, and other means of control are too slow to bring about elimination of the behavior, or (b) the behavior is self-reinforcing (e.g., eating, smoking, masturbation) so that ignoring it will have little or no effect.

Assume to begin with that punishment will be unnecessary in your classroom. Wait for the children to prove you wrong before considering punishment as the alternative. Even if you should have to use punishment, it will be only in rare and infrequent circumstances. Positive reinforcement should *always* be used more frequently.

5. You need to develop ways to count at least the most significant behaviors, especially those from the positive list. Choose whatever counting technique is easiest, as long as it is accurate; you should feel your management system is serving you rather than vice versa. Some pointers on counting:

(a) Behaviors that leave written evidence, such as number of worksheets completed, can still be counted when the children have left the classroom.

(b) Some behaviors can be observed at intervals (as far as recording is concerned). For example, keeping a running account of who is in-seat and for how long will be taxing; but you can use a kitchen timer, set it for varying lengths of time, and instruct the children to "freeze" when it sounds. Then a quick check can be made of where every one is and the children will enjoy the procedure as a game as well.

(c) If behaviors are well defined, almost anyone can count them, including the children. One of the privileges a good student could earn is being the behavior counter, or even the one who sets the timer.

(d) Your counting technique could be a part of the reward system, so that your records serve a double purpose. Your record sheet might cover a whole bulletin board and the tallies and stars (or other adhesive material) may be the only reinforcement you need to introduce.

(e) If you are secure in your consistency in counting throughout the day, you may need to count behavior for only a sample time span. For example, you may need to count for only an hour or half an hour to get an accurate record of what is happening throughout the day. Remember, you must collect an accurate and objective reading of *what is happening to the behavior(s) in question in order to correctly evaluate and change your program.*

(f) One last point. If you have never collected behavioral data on your children before, begin with only *one* behavior, and choose a conspicuous behavior. Don't discourage yourself by feeling overburdened. The process becomes surprisingly simple once you develop a system and an awareness of specific behaviors.

6. Now you are ready to begin construction. You have the building blocks and a way to be sure your plan is well constructed. Next, decisions need to be made concerning key questions.

(a) Exactly what behavior will you begin with? Let us suppose you choose in-seat behavior during a seatwork period that begins at 9:00 A.M. and ends at 10:30 A.M.

(b) How do you plan to count the behavior? If you choose to use a kitchen timer, you can set the timer for intervals ranging from 1 to 30 minutes with the average interval being 15 minutes. In this way, the children will never know when the timer will sound. The children are instructed to stay in place when the timer sounds until you tell them to continue. During this time you can quickly note those students who are out of their seats for inappropriate reasons. The counting procedure will certainly interrupt your routine, but not as much as the problem behavior you are trying to correct does. Also, as the timer proves to be successful in increasing desired behavior, you can gradually increase the mean number of minutes until eventually the timer sounds only two or three times during the period.

(c) Before you introduce any sort of consequence for appropriate behavior, try counting the behavior for a few days. This will give you information that is usually called *baseline* data. The baseline allows you the opportunity to compare what was happening before your program began with what happened during the program itself. An inappropriate program may do no good whatsoever, and without a baseline, the teacher will need more time to realize the lack of effect and more time to change the program.

(d) What will the *contingency program* (system of rewards) consist of? There are an endless number of alternatives and many important considerations. For example, you could choose a group contingency whereby appropriate behavior brings the entire class nearer a goal such as a party. While group contingencies are easier to administer, they may seem unfair to the students. If you are trying to reward in-seat behavior and one child doesn't bother to stay in his seat, his classmates will eventually earn the party reward without his assistance—but he, too, will attend the party. Individual contingencies are generally more fair, and generate fewer hard feelings and less competition and peer pressure.

You must also decide what the consequence itself will be. Quite probably there are consequences available in the classroom now such as class jobs, free time, games, and privileges. The consequence should match the children's level of sophistication and maturity. Candy may be appropriate for young children, or for exceptional children, but may be more juvenile than necessary for a group of fourth graders.

Lastly, you must be careful to structure the contingency program so that no one is left out. Simply by allowing children who don't have enough credit to save their credit, the slower children will have a head start when you begin working again. In this way, even the most hyperactive child will eventually be able to earn the reward for in-seat behavior. You might also wish to allow for a variety of rewards, so that you can individualize reinforcement as well as instruction.

Suppose you decide that a chart of the children's data for in-seat behavior, on an individual basis, will be adequate for reinforcement. (Later you may find the chart to be the center of interest during parent-teacher conferences, although that was not your initial objective in using the chart.) There is a risk in overemphasizing competition when you use such a visual display, but you feel the children will not suffer because, for a change, the quiet and timid will be able to excel. (The more energetic children already outdo the others in any competitive game or sport.) You use a bulletin board that is titled "Happy Hard Workers." At the left is a column containing the names of your second graders. The rest of the board is empty rows, one following each name. You have found a dime store that sells large bags of smiling face stickons. At the end of the seatwork period, you take a minute or so, just before recess when no one works anyway, to praise the children for their hard work. Then you (or a student helper, maybe the one who earned the most smiling faces yesterday) post as many smiling faces after each child's name as he has earned. If the stickers come in a variety of colors, you might also color code the days of the week. The smiling face is earned by being seated and apparently at work when the bell sounds. Since the children don't know when the bell will sound, they should feel motivated during the entire hour and a half period. You maintain daily records to detect whether or not the program is producing satisfactory results. Note that the number of timed periods will become fewer as time goes on. Therefore, you should make comparisons on the basis of the average number of children seated when the bell sounds rather than the average of in-seat children recorded for the entire day. (If you used the number for the entire day, the number would decrease simply because the number of bells decreased.)

A word of caution: the children will accept your data as motivating only if you are completely objective. You must not fail to notice that Mary is not in her seat just because she is your personal favorite. (Like it or not, we all have them.) And you must count John as in his seat if that's where he is when the bell sounds, despite the fact that he was moving all about the room for the ten minutes preceding the bell. Also, be sure to keep the time setting as random as possible. Otherwise, the socially intelligent child will quickly detect your pattern and will follow "the rule" only when it pays off.

(e) Every good formal reinforcement program should be good enough to be at least partly eliminated. The children behave as they do before the program because of the system of contingent rewards, no matter how subtle, that existed at that time. If you return to the same set of contingencies, eventually the behavior will become the same also. *There is no such thing as a habit maintained without reinforcement.* The children will not automatically remain in their seats once you feel they have the habit of doing so. But in all probability, they will need a less formalized program of reinforcement as time goes on. The teacher and her approval will be greatly strengthened in reinforcement value, and teacher approval alone may begin to replace the bulletin board chart, for example, as a conditioning technique.

The teacher may first lay the groundwork for using only approval as a reinforcer by giving oral praise to those who are working hard at their seats both when the timer bell goes off and during the intervals in between. The second step might be the removal of the bulletin board, with the same sort of record kept on an ordinary sheet of paper that is stored in the teacher's desk. Entries are made during recess and the children see the chart only when they ask about it. If the data suggests that the students' behavior deteriorates during this step, the teacher can move a half step backward by simply posting the sheet in the corner of a bulletin board. A third step would be to substitute slash marks for smiling faces on the chart and keep the record in the grade book. In step four, the teacher either gives a slash mark for good behavior or does not. In essence, the time period is now expanded to the whole hour and a half and the timer device can be eliminated.

Eventually, the teacher may make entries in her record book on a once-a-week basis, as she may already have done before the program began. It is important that the teacher maintain high rates of verbal reinforcement for in-seat behavior in order to assure the success of the behavioral program. Extinction will be used for any out-of-seat behavior that is not physically dangerous, and punishment for behavior that is dangerous. By the time teacher reaches step four, she is probably prepared to manage the next most important problem in the classroom.

PROGRAM GENERALIZATION

Generalization of appropriate in-seat behavior to other periods of the day may be considered throughout the program. The verbal praise that you use in conjunction with the program period as well as during other hours will be invaluable. Generalization increases in proportion to the similarity of stimuli. Therefore, when it is convenient to use some of the same stimuli, or some of the same program at other hours, do so.

You may also wish to avoid some of the program stimuli during periods when you want the children out of their seats in order to increase discrimination. Also, some teachers may feel children should be taught to adapt to both a highly structured and a highly unstructured class-room. Sometimes the children may be instructed to follow a list of rules. At other times there may be as few rules as possible. In order to increase discrimination between which condition the children are to respond to, the teacher should add a stimulus specifically for discrimination. (Remember, keeping stimuli more alike increases generalization.) For example, the teacher might play soft music or rearrange desks whenever the rules and formal contingencies for reward are not in effect, such as during crafts time or snack time. At all other times, the rules apply. The child in doubt could easily decide whether or not the rules were in effect.

The last point is very simple, but extremely valuable. You may well find that using extinction for disruptive behaviors may tax your patience and take too long. When you notice a child off-task, it's tempting to remind him of what he is supposed to be doing. *Don't do it!* You risk giving him positive reinforcement in the form of teacher attention. Instead, *look for the nearest child who is on-task, preferably a friend of the off-task child, and praise the on-task child for following directions.* In this way, you do not give attention to the off-task child, yet because he heard your praise of his friend he is reminded of what he's to do. You also identify a good model for him and further remind him that you will catch him being good rather than bad. Of course, you have also reinforced the on-task child and thereby strengthened his behavior.

REVIEW QUESTIONS

1. A social behavior differs from an academic behavior in that it is a behavior for which _____ .
2. The basic building blocks needed to create a management program are
   (a) _____
   (b) _____
   (c) _____
3. Punishment is only called for when
   (a) _____
   (b) _____
4. Creating the management program requires decisions about
   (a) What _____
   (b) How _____
   (c) How long to _____
   (d) What _____
   (e) How _____

CHAPTER **8**

The Academic Response

Every teacher interested in children is interested in far more than their social responses. Children are in school to learn skills, knowledge, and behavior that they do not already possess. However, a teacher cannot simply apply contingency principles of rewarding to create student behaviors that do not yet exist; if a behavior is not exhibited, it cannot be reinforced. It has become a cliché of education to say that "you must begin where the child is," at whatever level he has attained. Behavioral principles do not offer an alternative to this maxim. The methods of shaping and fading, described in Chapter 6, provide for teaching new behaviors through carefully planned series of steps, so that each successive step requires more than the preceding step. When the child progresses from one step to the next, either less help is provided, as in fading, or more skill is required, as in shaping. Principles for sequencing steps are most complex and vary according to child, teacher, and subject matter; therefore, no attempt will be made to explain these principles here. We will refer, though, to the curricular materials that conscientiously employ such principles—*programmed materials*. In these materials the steps for acquiring new knowledge or skills are carefully sequenced and are conspicuous, as in frames or lesson sequences. This chapter will emphasize the applicability of behavior modification to the academic response, and appropriate applications for already programmed materials will be suggested.

USING REWARDS WITH PROGRAMMED MATERIALS

If a teacher starts with curricular materials that are broken into carefully sequenced steps, behavioral principles become easy to apply. It is important that each step in the program has a well-defined beginning and end, so that rewards for desired behavior are available with each step. Operational short-term goals must be defined as well as long-term goals. For example, while the long-term goal may be learning to read orally certain lists of words with accuracy, the short-term goal may be completion of a specific exercise. Convenience is further served if the programmed steps or exercises require approximately equal time and effort to complete for ease in assignment and use in a contingency system.

A teacher could use time to work on the class project as a reward for the completion of required exercises. As an example, the project might be drawings of African scenery and animals which the class will compile in a book to supplement geography lessons. Each child has selected the topics for his drawings, and all the children seem enthusiastic about working on the book. The 90 minutes before morning recess are to be spent concentrating on reading activities and the first 20 minutes after recess on geography (not including the time needed to work on the project). For each reading exercise a student completes at 90 percent accuracy, he earns 10 minutes to work on the class project, such as the geography book, at the end of the reading period. In this way you know that every child will have something to do and those working on geography will be "warming-up" for the geography lesson. Your system will seem far more fair and consistent to the children if the exercises require approximately equal time and effort.

Note that the teacher in the example has made a fundamental assumption which may or may not be true for all the children—that working on the geography book is a reward. The reward is used to positively reinforce exercise completion in programmed material. If the assumption is wrong for an individual student because working on the book is aversive to him, the teacher will quickly discover this fact through the records of his performance on the exercises. Written academic behaviors are especially easy to record and graph. Should John's record indicate a decrease in exercise completion when the geography contingency is introduced, the teacher will see her error and can change the program, at least for John, in an effort to eliminate the error. The teacher may discover that she needs to think of some other way for John to contribute to the class project if he does not like to draw.

A fringe benefit of such a program is that the children are likely to enjoy working on the programmed exercise materials. In that case, the materials will be paired with reinforcement and should eventually become reinforcing themselves. The response of a class where programmed materials were used as part of the reward can be seen in this next example. After the children did their group math work, they went to their folders. The folders contained programmed material matched to each child's achievement. By completing the programmed lessons, the children earned points that could be exchanged for several different rewards. During most of the day, the folders remained in a filing cabinet that could easily be locked, and the teacher had the key. Whenever the noise level in the room began to grow too loud for the teacher, she would announce that unless the room was quiet, she would lock the cabinet. A locked cabinet meant no programmed materials for that day. Instantly the room became silent! The teacher was using negative reinforcement (removing an aversive threat contingent on no noise) when she could easily have used positive reinforcement for the quiet children, but the consequence worked because of the attraction of the rewards. The incident serves to demonstrate how much the children came to enjoy and look forward to their programmed study.

Formal reinforcement programs for academic behaviors require some individualization of instruction or antecedents. Without the individualization, the reward program will be grossly unfair to at least a few children. No class is truly homogeneous. Therefore, if you say that the pupils will get three points for completing math page 147, the points will be very easy for some children and very hard for others. Academically, especially, you must *reinforce the child's improved behavior relative to himself.* Doing so, requires individualization.

Not every teacher will have the financial resources to purchase quality programmed materials and very few teachers have the necessary training to make their own. Yet all instruction is programmed and sequenced to some degree. We generally teach history in chronological sequence, and arithmetic is taught before algebra. When the sequence is loosely defined, and the steps within the sequence are vague, a formal system of reinforcement is best avoided. Without clearly defined steps, and without everyone knowing where each step begins and ends, errors in reinforcement become predictable and conspicuous.

INFORMAL REWARDS

Informal programming calls for an informal reinforcement system. If Joey seems to have done exceptionally well in his oral reading, allow him time for some activity he especially enjoys. If slowpoke Mary finishes her math on time, praise her lavishly and suggest that she be first in line for recess. When timid Joan volunteers an answer to your question, call on her and praise her for her effort whether she's right or wrong. Concentrate on catching the children being good, not only socially but academically. *Catch 'em being smart!* Notice any good performance on the part of an individual child, and let him know you've noticed.

Use your imagination to find all the possible reinforcers in your class, and don't miss an opportunity to create more reinforcers than were originally there. Rather than going through a day looking only for errors, discover correct responses with enthusiasm and point them out to those responsible. Your enthusiasm will be appreciated, and extra privileges can be used to advantage in reinforcement. Extras might include feeding the gerbil or having the basketball at recess. Or you might have special extra honors so that when you spot an especially good paper you'll be able to reach in your pocket and put a big gold star on it, or hang it up on a special bulletin board, or put a quick plus behind the student's name in the grade book that you happened to have nearby. Soon the children will want to do schoolwork, and they'll want to show their work to you. As time goes on, they'll enjoy what they're doing—they'll enjoy school and they'll enjoy learning.

REVIEW QUESTIONS

1. The methods that allow for teaching new behaviors are called
   _____ and_____ .
2. When developing a formal program of reinforcement for academic responses, it is important that each step in the learning process have a well defined _____ and _____ .
3. According to _____ principles, materials paired with reinforcement will become reinforcing themselves.
4. When it comes to the academic response, catch 'em being _____ .

CHAPTER 9

Token Systems: Individualized Reinforcement

Individualization has become the motto of modern education. Instructional techniques that are directed at a group inevitably teach above some children and below others, whereas in individualized instruction every child is accepted at his own level and teaching progresses from that point. The trend toward reintegrating the exceptional child into the regular classroom is only one manifestation of the advantages of individualized instruction. If the teacher can individualize, it is no longer necessary to exclude the child who cannot fit into a reading group, or who cannot keep up with the class in math. The exceptional child studies skills appropriate for him, just as the other children do. Thus the fact that he is mildly retarded or learning disabled becomes less important, and the mildly handicapped child becomes less different from any other child in the classroom.

Teaching what the child is ready to learn is important, but hardly the whole job. The child must also experience consequences that are appropriate for him with respect to the task to be performed. We do not all like or dislike the same things. To further complicate matters, some things are liked or disliked only sometimes and the times are not always predictable. Mary will gladly work for the privilege of more time in the art corner because she loves to draw. But John dislikes art; he knows that he is less skilled at it than most of his classmates and it has become an aversion to him. Just as it seldom makes sense to teach a group as though all members had progressed to the same point, it seldom makes sense to reward all children in the same way as though they all liked the same things.

ADVANTAGES OF TOKEN SYSTEMS

The "naturally good" teacher individualizes reinforcement, and this requires a knowledge of each child's personality. Even when the teacher knows all the pupils very well, there will be errors in reinforcement because the children change in mood and need from day to day.

A token reinforcement system, or *token economy*, is a way to individualize reinforcement with minimal error. While other advantages will be mentioned, the individualization of reinforcement is the primary justification for the token system. The individualization becomes not only better, but easier, because the children choose their own rewards.

A token is defined as any symbol for reinforcement that can later be exchanged for another reinforcer.

The symbol itself may be anything from points in a grade book to gold stars or poker chips. Any reinforcement system that involves an exchange of tokens for some other reward is a token system.

Anyone who has worked for wages has experienced working in a token economy. Our token system can be observed in the following example. An employer may have several secretaries who do essentially the same job and who earn the same wage. One of the secretaries is a young woman who spends her money on clothes, makeup, and rent in the best singles apartment building in town; another is a working mother who saves her money for a down payment on a house; the third is an older woman who works to put her son through college; a fourth lives a miserly life in order to invest most of her check in the stock market. All the women have very different reinforcers for which they are willing to work. Yet all of them work hard and are reinforced with exactly the reward they want. Since they select the reward from among a huge variety of potential rewards, they inevitably choose something reinforcing. The reinforcement is completely individualized. Do you detect the token in the system here? Money is a token, a symbol exchangeable for other reinforcers. And the monetary system, international in scope, is the most extensive and complex token economy in existence. Without it, imagine how much time would be wasted on finding something for the employer to pay the employee and for the buyers to give the seller. Token systems, if well designed, can simplify rather than complicate an exchange.

"We all do the same job, but for different rewards. Yet no one feels cheated because we select our own rewards with our tokens."

DESIGNING TOKEN ECONOMIES

Let us consider how a token economy works in the classroom. A teacher has a class of twenty-eight fourth graders, with an equal number of boys and girls. The class is heterogeneous and samples different races, socioeconomic levels, and cultures. No rewards work for all the children all the time, not even traditional social reinforcement, grades, or evaluation. The children's ages range over three years and achievement levels vary even more. The brighter children would have many unfair advantages for reinforcement in group instruction, and individualization will eliminate this potential problem. The teacher was assigned the class because of previous experience with individualized instruction, and has realized that this type of instruction required individualized rewards to be most effective.

Token systems tend to encourage the teacher to individualize instruction since the system is likely to be unfair in a group-instruction setting. Here are the steps involved in designing token economies:

1. The teacher makes a list of everything that could be used as a reward in the classroom, including in the list items that are already available and others that would require little cost or trouble to obtain. Among the items on the list are grades, games, classroom jobs, privileges such as being first in line, visiting other classes, going to the library or gym, reading to the class or to the principal, working in the art or science corner, candy, certificates of achievement, complimentary letters to parents, stars for individual charts, and class supplies such as colored paper and pencils.

2. She assigns a point value to each item on the list. In doing so she is subjective, but does try to look at the list from both the child's point of view and her own. She knows that errors made at this step will become evident later, because "overpricing" (in terms of token points) will result in too few children "purchasing" the item, and "underpricing" will result in too many. When such errors become evident, she reserves the right to alter the "price" accordingly.

3. She edits the list so that it does not become too long and confusing. Yet, she knows her children well enough to know that there are at least several items that are likely to appeal to each one of her students. The list that results from the editing is called the *menu*. Technically you can design a token system with only one reward and no menu, but doing so eliminates the greatest advantage, choice of reward.

4. Another list is needed. The teacher lists all those behaviors that she would like to reward, which range from the student's sitting quietly in his seat and not crying when he fails, to assignment completion, good oral reading, and correct answers on quizzes. In other words, the teacher includes both social and academic behaviors on the list.

5. Again, point values are assigned to the behaviors on the list. The teacher may wish to assign a range of point values so that she can take unpredictable variables into account. On some days it is harder for a student to stay in his seat, and on some days it's harder to complete an assignment. Just before Christmas, it may be especially hard to study for a test. The teacher may also make some exceptions to the list of behavior; for example, if Maria is reading at the second-grade level but doing arithmetic at the fifth-grade level, it might be a good idea to award Maria more points than the others for reading behaviors and fewer points for math.

6. More editing. The list must be condensed to avoid confusing the children. To begin with, only two or three behaviors should be included on the list, and other behaviors can be added as the children adjust to the system.

7. The token itself must be selected and a record-keeping system devised. Since the children are fourth graders, the teacher feels secure in using an abstract token. She has chosen points for the token and records the points on a chart posted behind her desk; or charts could be put on each child's desk and points added by the teacher as she attends to each child.

8. An exchange system must be devised that is minimally distracting. Once a child earns points, when and how can he exchange them? The process is likely to be easier if the exchange takes place only at certain times during the day or week. Disruptions will be further minimized if potentially noisy items, such as free time, are only available for purchase during the last period of the day. The teacher decides to have exchange time (to open the store) at 2:30 P.M. every day, just 45 minutes before school is out, and items like free time and game playing are limited to the 30 minutes immediately following the exchange. Other items such as errand runners are purchased for the next day. When a child makes a purchase, the teacher simply crosses out the appropriate number of points on the chart.

9. Lastly, the teacher must devise a tentative plan for phasing out the token point system. She feels that eventually she would only like to give points for written work, and the points would be used for grades, privileges, and class projects. She knows that by gradually overpricing other items, she will eventually be able to shorten the list because overpricing will inhibit purchasing. Then she can announce to the class, "No one has purchased candy for several weeks, so I'm going to remove it from the menu," or "Sorry, since no one purchased any, I've stopped buying candy."

By simply praising children who exhibit good social behaviors, she will be able to award fewer and fewer points for that behavior. However, her rate of praise for social behaviors must remain high, especially after the points have been removed entirely. Removal of point giving must be very gradual and consistent for all class members. Eventually, the point chart can take a different form, too. It can be rewritten on an 8 × 11-inch sheet of paper and taped to her desk. Next, the teacher can remove the point sheet entirely and keep the record only in her grade book.

EXTRAS

There are a number of additional benefits to using classroom token economies. First, a well-designed token system at work in the classroom helps to develop positive classroom management. If you find yourself catching kids being bad more than you catch them being good, a positive token system will change that. The concrete nature of such a plan will also increase consistency in teacher behavior. A token system will help you overcome inconsistencies in managing children because any inconsistencies will be evident to you and the children.

Second, a token system can be used to teach math skills. Teachers of young children are frequently amazed at the money-counting skills of children who, they thought, couldn't add. Math, like any other subject, is easier when it is made relevant and concrete. Imagine how easy it would be to tell the children in a class that they cannot make a purchase until they tell the teacher what their total number of points is and how many points they will have left after subtracting the amount of the purchase. Other concepts such as change making, check cashing, savings accounts, inflation, and devaluation could also be taught using token points. Token systems can teach abstract math concepts such as the value of savings. For example, suppose free time is one of the rewards; for 5 tokens, the child can earn 5 minutes, but for 20 tokens, he can earn 30 minutes of free time. Before long, the child who has never saved for anything in his life will save his tokens.

Third, the prospect of earning token points helps the child understand the marking system—it shows him how he earns his grade. Token systems are especially useful in offsetting the behavior of the child who must blame others and usually selects the teacher as his target while in school. Many children, particularly the slow learners and the emotionally disturbed, will not have developed an internal locus of control; that is, some children explain all that happens to them on the basis of what others do, not what they do themselves. Seldom will such children understand that a low grade, for example, is the result of not studying. These children may need help in understanding that they can affect what happens to them in school. Their behavior can make the teacher's day miserable, yet few teachers know how to change such a mental set. When the classroom privileges and honors are listed on a menu, and exactly how the children can earn tokens for them is explained, the children soon discover that they can control at least part of their fate.

Fourth, many children need structure in order to be comfortable and able to learn. Other children can benefit greatly from a more flexible classroom structure where they must make decisions for themselves. A token system can allow for service to both needs simultaneously.

Any child who is chronologically younger or mentally less mature, who is easily distracted, or who is simply in an unfamiliar environment will benefit from added classroom structure. For example, children with learning disabilities or minimal brain damage are said to be in special need of structure and any consequence that confirms the fact that the child is or has been on-task is desirable. The learning-disabled child seems to become confused by the sensory bombardment he experiences in class, and a consistent and conspicuous reinforcer, such as a star on the chart taped to his desk, will serve as a guide to the child. When he sees a star added to his chart, it will positively endorse his perceptions of what he is doing. A hyperactive and distractible child will also be reminded of what he is supposed to be doing when he sees another child receive reinforcement. The tokens become concrete guideposts for many children. Language is abstract, invisible, and transient in its sensory impact, and many children need more than verbal guideposts.

While the "average" child needs both structured and unstructured periods, above average and creative children should be allowed additional freedom in order to develop their assets. The menu can easily be adapted to provide alternatives, including many that are open ended. For example, you may have ten items on the menu, and one of them is time to work in the art or science corner. Both of these activity corners contain materials that allow for hundreds of activities for the child who has a quick and creative mind. Another item may be library time, so that a gifted child may choose to complete his work quickly, collect his tokens, and check out for the library. Once there, he is limited only by the facility. Free time on the menu is yet another way to serve the creative child. In effect, the menu that seemed to include only ten items may really include hundreds. The open-ended choices expand the menu to the limits of the children's ability to imagine.

RESTORING POSITIVE REINFORCEMENT

In Chapter 4 a young teacher with a third-grade class she thought was "out to get her" was described. Miss Brown's class was chaotic, despite her generally positive approach to the children, because she reinforced them at all the wrong times for all the wrong things. In-service training in the use of a classroom token system helped the teacher be consistent and make appropriate rewards.

Miss Brown made errors in social reinforcement by attending in a positive way to undesirable behavior. Explaining these reinforcement errors to her proved to be ineffective. Therefore, a token system was designed that relied on a different kind of reward—tangible and consumable rewards. In this way, the possibility that the teacher's inappropriate attention-giving habits might interfere with the token system was avoided. The rewards were candy: M&M's and bridge mix in a box marked 5, suckers and other penny candy in a box marked 10, and small boxes containing eight to ten pieces of candy corn or baked beans in a box marked 20.

The tokens were made from orange posterboard cut into 1-inch squares, then stamped with a symbol so that the children could not duplicate the squares. (Round tokens require a great deal of work if you make them yourself.)

Study periods were divided into segments that were initially about 5 minutes long; a kitchen timer was used to mark the intervals. By the end of the first morning the intervals were expanded to an average of 15 minutes, but varied from 1 to 30 minutes in length.

Four classroom rules were developed from a meeting of the class observers with the teacher. These were worded as positively as possible and placed by Miss Brown on the blackboard. They read as follows:

1. Remain seated unless you have permission
2. Remain silent unless you have permission
3. Raise your hand to get permission
4. Do your work as best you can

The last rule was to avoid reinforcing a child who simply sat and did nothing.

On the first day of the token system, the new procedure was explained to the children. The timer would be set. When it went off, each child who had kept the rules during that period would receive a token. If the child had broken a rule(s), he would receive a slip of paper with the number of the rule(s) but no token. At the end of the morning, tokens could be exchanged for candy. Five tokens could buy one piece from the 5 box, ten could buy one piece from the 10 box, and twenty could buy one piece from the 20 box. The boxes were clear plastic to allow the children to see inside.

Data was collected on out-of-seat behavior, because children in their seats would eliminate most of Miss Brown's problems. Before the program, the children left their chairs from 60 to 80 times during 30-minute observation periods. After the program began, that data was always less than 20 children per 30 minutes. The room was far more quiet, though no attempt was made to measure the noise.

The system also taught the children to save since more tokens bought more candy per token. But there was a problem: Miss Brown had difficulty keeping up with the children. Many children finished the prepared curriculum long before the end of the day.

Candy became an unsatisfactory reward. Many of Miss Brown's fellow teachers disapproved of using candy as a reward in a classroom, so that more acceptable rewards were needed. Fortunately (and at about the same time we observers wanted to suggest them) Miss Brown asked suggestions for alternative rewards. A menu was developed for classroom privileges and the most expensive item was being the token distributor for a day, 50 tokens. Candy was left on the menu, but was seldom purchased. One day it was removed and the children did not notice the deletion.

Other changes occurred. Miss Brown developed new confidence in herself and began to trust the children. She planned field trips and art projects that would not have been considered before the system was introduced.

SUMMING UP

There is nothing magical about a token system. Understand it for what it is: concrete symbolic reinforcement exchangeable for other reinforcers. The advantages are several, but if you and your class will not benefit from the advantages, forget the token system. Certainly, not every classroom calls for one. The advantages of a token system:

1. Provides individualization in reinforcers.
2. Expands the reinforcing alternatives. You cannot let John read to the principal or go on a field trip every time he reads well orally. But you can give him a token, which will eventually lead to the purchase of such privileges.
3. Facilitates the addition of structure and/or unstructured time to the classroom routine, depending upon need.
4. Offers prompt reinforcement. A reward will be far more likely to affect behavior when it is introduced very soon after the behavior. By using tokens, the teacher may reinforce a child with the prospect of an event that will not take place until the end of the day.

5. Adds variety and excitement to the classroom, and enhances positive classroom management.

REVIEW QUESTIONS

1. What is a token?
2. A bonus side effect of a token economy is that it can be used to teach _____
3. Miss Brown's fundamental error was that she _____
4. List five fundamental reasons for using a token system.

Schedules of Reinforcement: How To Be Efficient

THINNING THE SCHEDULE

When a program of reinforcement is initiated, it is most common and almost always appropriate to reinforce the child for each performance of the desired behavior. When teaching baby to say "milk," you would certainly give baby milk the first time he says the word. When you want Johnny to sit on his chair for five consecutive minutes (he very rarely has before) and he finally makes it, you would certainly reinforce him. When Mary first finishes her reading assignment on the same day it is assigned, you reinforce her without hesitation.

As time goes on, and the child becomes very adept at the behavior, it will become inefficient, and possibly inappropriate, to reinforce every performance of the behavior. Instead, consider thinning the schedule of reinforcement. Once baby says "milk" so well that he says it too often during the day, you may wish to reinforce the behavior *only at the right time* such as mealtime. When Johnny learns to sit down for long periods of time, it may serve no purpose and may interrupt his studying if you walk over and reinforce him *every* five minutes. Once Mary finishes her assignment in the same amount of time or less than her peers, it may be inappropriate to attend to her more than to the others.

The concept of thinning schedules of reinforcements is related to the process of phasing out token systems. Once a token system is introduced and successful, the teacher should begin to consider ways of making the token system more closely approximate the usual contingencies provided in the school system. That is, tokens should be gradually phased out as the purpose of prompt rewards for desired school behavior has been served, assuming that there are traditional school reinforcers that can replace those of the token system. Thinning schedules of reinforcement is almost always one of the steps in the phaseout of a token economy.

In the example with the child learning to talk, we saw that a mother would always reinforce the baby saying "milk" with milk, then change to reinforcing the behavior only at mealtime; mother has thinned the schedule based on time of day. Johnny sits in his seat for longer and longer periods of time before he is reinforced; the schedule is thinned based on the passage of time. Mary's case is different. She hands in assignments on time and her schedule of reinforcement would probably be thinned based on the *frequency* of the behavior. First she was reinforced for each assignment; later she may be reinforced on an average of once for two assignments, then one to three, and so on.

Schedules may be thinned on a time-dependent basis or on a frequency-dependent basis. *There are four fundamental kinds of schedules and each will affect the behavior in a different way. Therefore, it makes sense to select a schedule on the basis of the effect you wish to produce on the behavior.* The four schedules are called fixed interval, variable interval, fixed ratio, and variable ratio. The first two depend on the passage of time, the second two on the frequency of the behavior.

TIME-DEPENDENT SCHEDULES

Fixed intervals and variable intervals.   In a *fixed interval* schedule, reinforcement for a behavior becomes available after time periods whose lengths are equal. A *variable interval* schedule is essentially the same, except that the lengths of the time periods vary. Yet the effects of the two schedules are quite different.

Suppose you are a high-school history teacher. You want to reinforce studying behavior on the part of your students. You decide to create quizzes that are easy enough so that with minimal study efforts students will pass, but without study they will fail. The quizzes are graded on a pass-fail basis. You decide to use a fixed interval schedule, and you announce that there will be a quiz every Friday. What you have said is that you will provide the opportunity for reinforcement of studying (passing) after fixed periods of time, or every seven days. Of course you've also created the same schedule for negative reinforcement, that is, studying to avoid failing. As you can imagine, very few studying behaviors will occur on Saturday or Sunday. But there will also be little studying done on Monday, and only slightly more on Tuesday. By

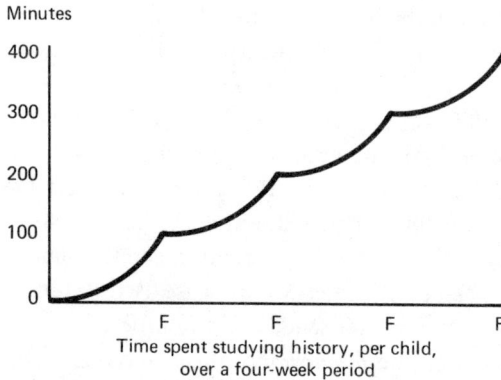

FIGURE 10. Cumulative graph for studying behavior on a fixed interval schedule.

Wednesday, there will be more studying, and by Thursday, there will be lots of studying. A cumulative graph of the studying behavior would show a curious scalloped design. The same design would be found for any behavior on a fixed interval schedule of reinforcement. (See Figure 10.)

All of us respond to fixed interval schedules. Grades are usually awarded on fixed intervals. Late evening socializing is also usually at fixed intervals (weekends). Christmas present buying and income tax reporting are also fixed (annual). Anything that is scheduled daily, weekly, or annually is likely to produce some fixed schedules of reinforcement.

As a history teacher, suppose you want students to study a little every night rather than more and more as the Friday quiz approaches. All you need to do is change the schedule of reinforcement. One way to change the schedule is to give unannounced quizzes, which occur at a variable interval schedule of reinforcement. You may have exactly the same number of quizzes, an average of one per week. The quizzes may be neither easier nor harder than the announced quizzes, yet studying will be distributed more or less evenly over each week night. Friday and Saturday will continue to be exceptions because you cannot quiz on Saturday or Sunday.

What has changed is the student's ability to predict when the reinforcement for studying will be available. You may test two weeks after the last test, or the next day! Nobody knows but you. Therefore, it makes no sense for students to study history more on Thursday than on Monday. To maximize reinforcement, the student must study consis-

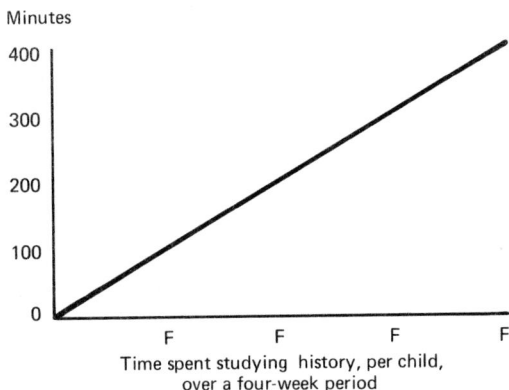

FIGURE 11.   Cumulative graph for studying behavior on a variable interval schedule.

tently. The curve, then, for a variable interval schedule of reinforcement approximates a straight line. The scallops are eliminated. (See Figure 11.)

There are many variable interval schedules of reinforcement in all of our lives. If you care to find those affecting you, look for behaviors that occur at slow, but very consistent rates. Many of us take time to dress neatly and groom ourselves because we never know when we might get complimented. We put money in parking meters or we check for chalk on our tires in relaxed but consistent ways, because we never know when the meter maid may walk down the street where we've parked; (notice that the behavior here is negatively reinforced, but reinforced nevertheless). If there was a video camera focused on your teaching behavior that could be turned on in the school office at *any time*, your teaching would be consistently good. You would have no way of predicting when a peer, parent, or principal was watching. The time interval between observations would vary in an unpredictable way.

FREQUENCY-DEPENDENT SCHEDULES

The other two basic schedules are controlled by behavioral frequency rather than timing. As one might expect, behavior that is reinforced on a frequency basis produces faster and sometimes frenzied rates of responding. Such schedules are called ratio schedules; that is, there exists some ratio of behaviors to each reinforcer. If the teacher says to Jack, "For each set of five math problems completed correctly, I will give you a point," then the schedule is set on a *ratio* of five behaviors to one reinforcer, or 5:1.

Fixed and variable ratio schedules. Ratio schedules can be divided into two types, fixed and variable, just as in interval schedules. The example with Jack and his arithmetic is a *fixed ratio* schedule because the reinforcer is always contingent on exactly five behaviors. If the teacher had said, "I'll give you a point for varying numbers of problems, but the points will average out to one point for five problems," the schedule would have been *variable ratio* at 5:1.

Let us examine fixed ratio schedules more closely. Any schedule that resembles "piece work" payment is a fixed schedule. Examples of such schedules are commonplace both in the world of employment and in the classroom. (Social reinforcers are almost never on fixed ratio schedules.) Consider the following fixed ratios:

"You will receive a $50 bonus for each $1,000 worth of merchandise you sell."

"With four magazine subscriptions, you get a fifth free."

"With the purchase of three tires (already on sale!) you get the fourth for half price."

"Buy one, get the second for one cent."

"For each set of 10 gears you assemble, you will be paid $1.00."

"For every 25 telephone books you deliver, you will be paid $1.50."

"As your book order increases by units of 100, the price will be 5% less than the previous price issued."

Some examples of fixed ratios in the classroom:

"For each set of three words you recognize today, and that you didn't know yesterday, you may have a free period (10 minutes)."

"When you finish your seatwork (always five pages) you may go to the library."

"When you complete 10 frames in your programmed reader, I will give you a ticket for the puppet show."

"For each 10-page essay you write at home, you may add 2 points to your lowest test score."

"Whenever you get three 100's on the spelling quizzes, you may skip the next spelling quiz."

"If you get five 'extra work' math papers done at 90% accuracy or better, Mr. Brown will allow you to swim during gym time."

"If you follow my directions without help on the art project on five occasions, Miss Jones (who teaches the next highest grade and is well liked) will let you take an art period in her room!"

All of us are affected by fixed schedules. Just as with fixed interval schedules, fixed ratios produce an interesting pattern, and the individual knows when he will get reinforced. "If I do this X number of times, I get Y." "If I do 10 problems correctly, I get another point." What do you suppose Johnny does as soon as he finishes the tenth problem? Will he begin the eleventh problem as quickly as he began the ninth? No. When he finishes the tenth problem he probably will respond with a sigh of relief, and pause to scratch his head, look out the window, talk to a friend, or raise his hand to attract teacher attention. After awhile he'll get around to doing the eleventh problem and will continue full-speed ahead until he finishes the twentieth problem. Then another pause. You can witness this sort of pausing behavior in any fixed ratio schedule. The behavior is "all or nothing," with the nothing periods coming right after the reinforcement.

The pause may be very brief or quite lengthy depending upon the difficulty of the task, the degree to which the schedule has been thinned, and satiation for the reinforcer. The easier the task, the shorter the pause. The thinner the schedule, for example 10 behaviors for one reward rather than three behaviors, the longer the pause. The greater the reinforcer satiation, the longer the pause. (After you get the second bottle of aspirin free, or the fourth tire at half price, you are not likely to be very interested in more aspirin or tires, even if they are a good buy.)

The pattern for fixed ratio schedules, then, is stepped. Our graph in the example for doing math problems might look something like the one shown in Figure 12; the horizontal lines in the graph represent pauses.

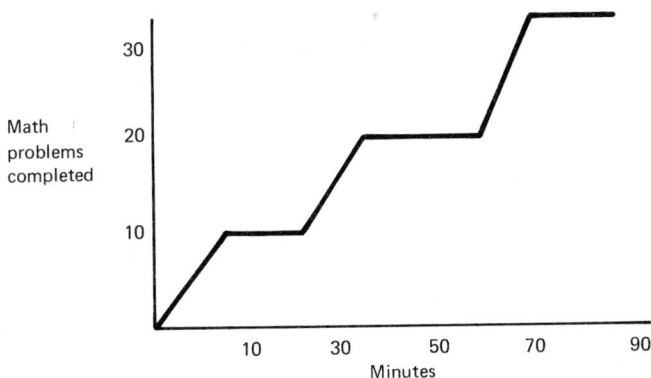

FIGURE 12. An example of a graph for a fixed ratio schedule.

If you want to avoid pauses on the behavior, fixed ratio scheduling of reinforcement is not a good idea. If you want the behavior to continue at very high, consistent rates, variable ratio is the schedule for you.

Suppose four poker sharks are playing poker. All the players are equally skilled, and we can assume that winning is basically a matter of chance. There are four players, so the chance of winning any single game is one in four. Assume that winning is the reinforcer for which each of the players is playing. Each player knows that he will not win exactly once every four games (that would be a fixed ratio); winning will only *average* one in four games. A player may win several consecutive games, or may not win for twenty or thirty games! The schedule varies and is a function of how many games are played. It is a variable ratio schedule of reinforcement. Now recall the last time you watched a group of real card sharks play; remember how *fast* they played, and how impatient the players became if someone was slow. Pauses were rare, and occurred only when there was no choice. All real gambling behaviors are on variable ratio schedules of reinforcement. In fact, all behaviors maintained on this schedule tend to "feel like" gambling behaviors. The performer knows that the number of times he performs the behavior is important for reinforcement, yet he doesn't know *which* one behavior will result in reinforcement. Each behavior is like taking a chance on a payoff.

Consider the salesman who works on commission. Each customer is a potential payoff. Yet only a few customers buy his goods. He doesn't know when he might find a purchaser, so he waits on as many customers as he can. When the merchandise is expensive, as in furniture or automobiles, he's likely to offer his card so that if the customer should change his mind, he'll go back to the original salesman. If such stores didn't assign salesmen to customers on a rotating basis, one might even see salesmen fighting over the chance to serve a customer. Sales behavior is maintained at a very high and consistent rate. One can see similar behavior in people who frequent sales, especially rummage sales. You never know which sale will have the terrific bargain, so you go to as many as you can as often as you can.

Except for many games, there are relatively few variable ratio schedules of reinforcement in the classroom. Perhaps this is because behavior consistently maintained at such high frequencies is not desirable. Or, more likely, it's because teachers have not given the idea much thought.

Suppose you had been giving Johnny a point for each set of 10 problems he completed. He would be working on a fixed ratio. To change to a variable ratio, imagine putting 100 slips of paper in a bag. When Johnny finishes a problem he may grab a slip. Ten of the slips have the number 1 on them. The other 90 are blank. If Johnny gets a slip with a 1 written on it, he gets a point; if not, he doesn't. The slips are constantly returned to the bag. The ratio of reinforcement to problem-solving behavior remains 10:1, but now Johnny doesn't know which behavior will pay off. The schedule has become variable. Assuming that he is interested in accumulating points, his math problem-solving behavior should remain at a high rate, but with fewer pauses.

The creative teacher should be able to think of many similar ways to create variable ratio schedules, especially for written academic behaviors where the behavior is easily counted and recorded. Bulletin boards could be utilized for "games of chance," where students earn the turn to take a chance by completing work. Payoffs would remain unpredictable. One teacher used a pointer mounted on a large board; the pointer could be spun and would eventually stop at a number from 1 to 20. Certain numbers paid off with certain privileges, and most numbers had no payoff at all. When a student completed a project before a due date, he was allowed to spin the pointer. Variable ratio schedules have a way of adding excitement to any situation. Therefore, some use of such schedules, especially for subjects or times which seem a bit boring, might be useful to any teacher.

In summary, schedules of reinforcement can be used to maintain behavior at slow, consistent rates (variable interval) or high consistent rates (variable ratio). "Scalloped" rates of behavior are created with fixed interval schedules. Behavior that comes in spurts with intermittent pauses is maintained by a fixed ratio schedule. Whatever schedule the teacher selects in the classroom, it should be done with the effect of the schedule in mind.

REVIEW QUESTIONS

1. What are the four fundamental schedules of reinforcement?
2. A *ratio schedule* means that reinforcement is dependent upon _____ . An *interval schedule* means that reinforcement is dependent upon _____ .
3. What effects do each of the four types of schedules tend to have on a given behavior?

PART II
Sample Projects

Introduction

The following twenty studies were done by teachers in their own class-rooms. The studies were selected because of their clear, simple design, the good results obtained from the studies, and because their subject matter is likely to be of interest to a great many teachers.

The design of the experiments is consistent in all the studies. Each teacher defined a behavior of great concern in such a way that the behavior could be easily counted. Then the teacher counted the behavior for several days prior to initiating the intervention program. *This pre-intervention time is called baseline, or A_1.* Baseline allows for comparing the intervention technique to that period of time before the technique was used.

The intervention period is referred to here as B (or B_1) and comes after A_1. The intervention that takes place is the plan that the teacher formulated to remediate the behavior in question in order to approximate a behavioral objective. During intervention, the teacher continued counting the same behavior.

The last phase of the experimental design is often called a reversal, or a return to the conditions of baseline. However, since this phase approximates A_1, *it can be abbreviated to A_2.* This last phase allowed the teacher to observe and count the behavior after the intervention procedures were removed. If the behavior again deteriorated during A_2, the teacher usually chose to reinstate intervention.

Most of the studies in these sample projects do not report data during *reinstatement, B_2.* The teachers simply discontinued the careful data collection during reinstatement because they already knew how effective the intervention had proven to be.

If no deterioration occurred during A_2, teachers often assumed that students had found new reinforcers for their improved behavior and that the reinforcers of intervention were no longer necessary.

The experimental design used here follows A_1, B, A_2. The intervention program (B) can be compared to what existed before (A_1) and after (A_2) in order to assess its effectiveness. Any teacher can incorporate this simple design in the teaching schedule to investigate the effectiveness of various intervention programs that could be used in the classroom.

The studies are arranged so that those involving young children appear first. Chronological age increases through the senior high school level from the first to the last of the studies.

CLASS: First Grade
BEHAVIOR: Visits to Health Room

CIRCUMSTANCES
The subject for this study is a six-year-old girl in the first grade who had numerous complaints about her health and who consequently made frequent visits to the school health room.

TARGET BEHAVIOR
Subject made visits to health room several times each week.

BEHAVIORAL OBJECTIVE
No visits to the school health room within an entire school day.

EXPERIMENTAL DESIGN

A_1 2 weeks
B 6 weeks
A_2 2 weeks

INTERVENTION
The program involved the use of graphing. A star was awarded to the subject each day she did not go to the health room. The stars were put on a chart posted in front of the room. No back-up reinforcer was used. Peer approval accompanied the star presentation.

RESULTS
Number of daily visits to school health room (see Figure 13).

	Mean	Median
A_1	1.6	1.5
B	.3	0.0
A_2	.1	0.0

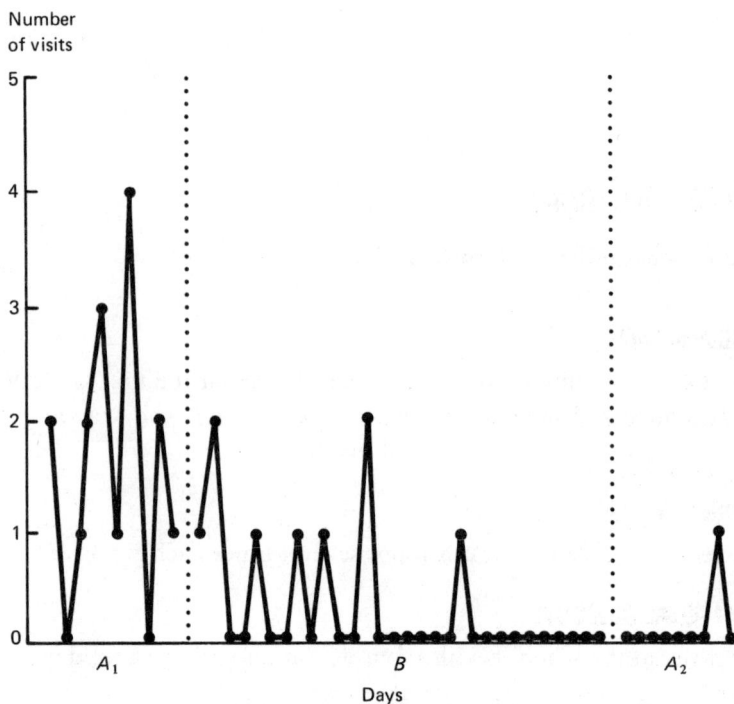

FIGURE 13. Visits to the health room, from A_1 to A_2.

EVALUATION

The objective was accomplished. Health complaints were reduced along with a reduction in visits to health room.

IMPLICATIONS

for the use of behavior modification materials: Graphing forms.

OTHER MATERIALS

that might have been useful: Contract forms and token materials.

CLASS: First grade
BEHAVIOR: Accurate Reading Worksheet Completion

CIRCUMSTANCES
The subjects for this study were five girls and three boys in the first grade who were in the lowest reading group.

TARGET BEHAVIOR
Children made careless errors in reading skills workbooks. The teacher counted the number of worksheets completed without error each day.

BEHAVIORAL OBJECTIVE
To increase the number of workbook pages that were completed without error in a given work period each morning.

EXPERIMENTAL DESIGN

A_1	10 days
B_1	15 days
A_2	5 days
B_2	8 days

INTERVENTION
During baseline and reversal periods (A_1 and A_2), token reinforcement was not given for the appropriate on-task behavior. After completing an assignment, the children went to the teacher who checked their work. If there were mistakes, the children went back to their desks and corrected them. Some children were very careless because they could fix errors with little difficulty.

When beginning intervention, the teacher displayed a tagboard chart. The children were shown how to correct their own papers using the teacher's manual. While checking the papers, they used a felt pen that made cheating impossible. A child, after completing an assignment accurately, was allowed to put a smiling-face token after his name on the chart. At the end of each week during the program, the child with the most smiling faces was given a certificate of achievement. In case of ties, those involved all received certificates. The certificates were brightly colored and decorated along the edges; they could be displayed or taken home. A "champion" was identified at the end of the three-week intervention period. The champ was awarded a prize which turned out to be a Sesame Street activity book.

RESULTS

The number of assignments finished without error was as follows.

	Mean	Median
A_1	10	10
B_1	28.6	23
A_2	15	7.5
B_2	21	21

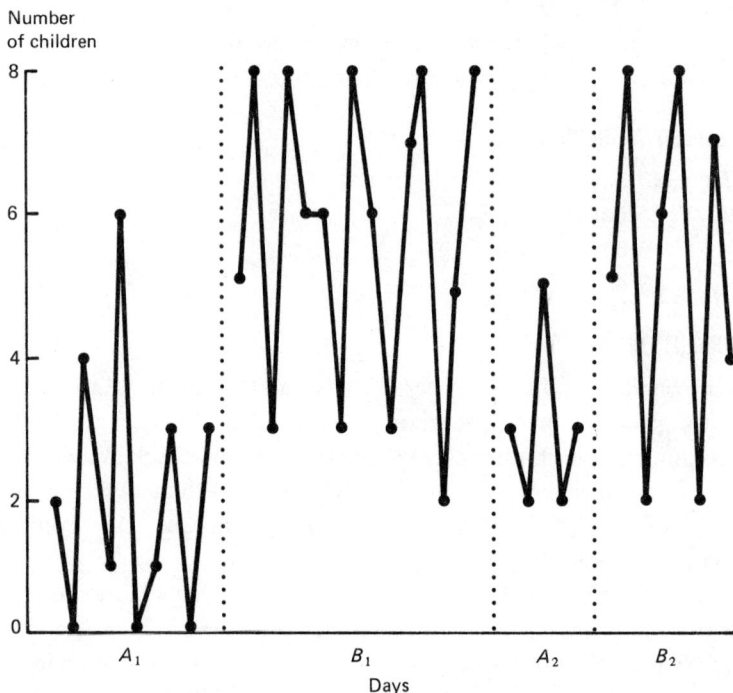

FIGURE 14. Number of children who completed assignments without making errors, from baseline (A_1) to reinstatement. (B_2).

EVALUATION

The objective was accomplished. Error-making behavior decreased during the reversal period, indicating the worth of the program (see Figure 14).

Implications for the use of behavior modification materials: Graphing forms for the chart, token materials (smiling faces), and certificates.

Other materials that might have been useful: Contract forms and premiums.

CLASS: First grade
BEHAVIOR: Turning in Accurate Papers

CIRCUMSTANCES

The classroom contained twenty-six first-grade students. One child had been labeled emotionally disturbed and another learning disordered by the school psychologist. All children were five- to seven-years old, and all had 45 minutes to do seatwork assignments each day.

TARGET BEHAVIOR

To increase the number of accurate papers turned in daily by the children. To be *accurate*, a paper had to be 90 percent correct.

BEHAVIORAL OBJECTIVE

To significantly increase the number of seatwork papers turned in that were 90 percent accurate in a given three-week intervention period.

EXPERIMENTAL DESIGN

A_1 15 days
B 14 days
A_2 10 days

INTERVENTION

Originally, the children were allowed to read a book or draw a picture if the seatwork was finished. If the child didn't finish the seatwork, he sometimes got a pep talk and took it home for homework.

During intervention, the teacher made "Snoopy money." The child received $100.00 in Snoopy money for each accurate assignment he completed. With the play money, he could buy the following rewards.

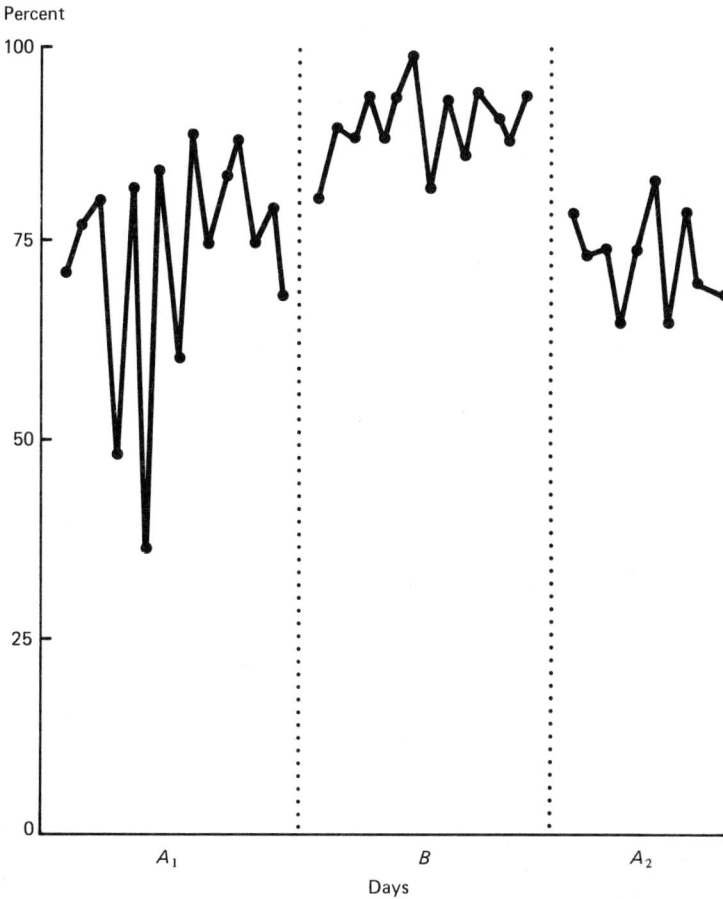

FIGURE 15. Percent of assignments complete and 90 percent accurate, A_1 to A_2.

Options	Snoopy Money
1. Use a tiles game	$300.00
2. Play with puzzles	300.00
3. Take a ball out at recess	400.00
4. Get a pass to come into school early	700.00
5. Be captain at the listening center	700.00
6. Select story at story time	800.00
7. Use easel	800.00
8. Play the "Winnie the Pooh" game	800.00
9. Visit another teacher's room	900.00

Since the number of assignments varied from day to day, the teacher calculated the percent of completed accurate assignments of those possible for a given day (see Figure 15).

RESULTS

Figures represent the percent of papers turned in and 90 percent accurate for the whole class.

	Mean	Median
A_1	74%	78%
B	88	88.5
A_2	73	72.5

EVALUATION

The teacher felt the intervention program was highly successful because

1. The percentage of accurate assignments went up greatly during intervention
2. The teacher needed to do much less nagging, give fewer pep talks, etc.
3. The students learned something about addition and subtraction using Snoopy money
4. The teacher was forced to stay up-to-date on paper correcting
5. Other teachers in the school began using similar programs
6. It was fun

Implications for use of behavior modification materials: Tokens, menus, high-interest activities.

CLASS: Open Classroom
BEHAVIOR: In-Seat Posture

CIRCUMSTANCES

The child was a seven-year-old boy. He was placed in a team-taught open classroom with forty-four other first graders. The child had no physical or mental disabilities.

TARGET BEHAVIOR

The child in question was not observing in-seat posture for the 30-minute quiet seatwork period each day. *In-seat* was defined as having some part of his body in physical contact with the desk.

BEHAVIORAL OBJECTIVE

To increase the number of 5-minute periods that the child remained in his seat during a two-week intervention program.

EXPERIMENTAL DESIGN

A_1 5 days
B 11 days
A_2 3 days

INTERVENTION

For every 5 minutes during the 30-minute seatwork period that the child remained in his seat, he received a square of orange tape with adhesive backing. The adhesive tape was then attached to a graph. The graph had 10 columns for 10 days, and 6 rows for the 5-minute units in 30 minutes. To completely fill his graph for a particular day, the child had to earn 6 squares of tape. The graph was only a visual record of the child's behavior. There were no back-up reinforcers for which the graph could be exchanged. Verbal approval accompanied the adhesive squares.

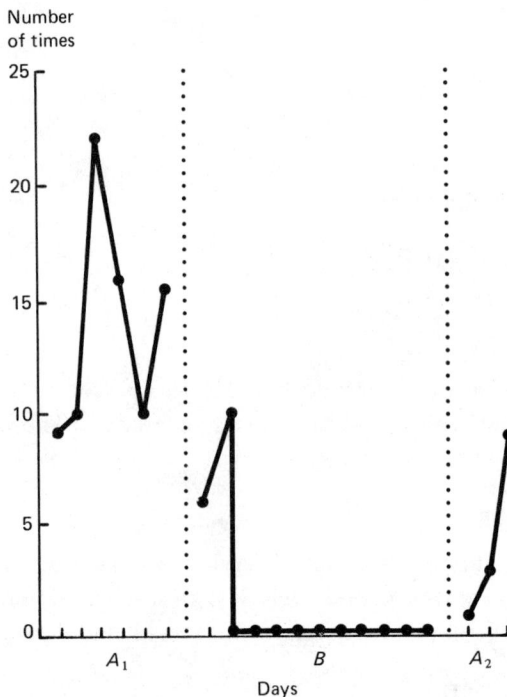

FIGURE 16.   Number of times out of seat in 30-minute seatwork periods, A_1 to A_2.

RESULTS

The mean number of times the child left his seat during the three experimental periods was as follows.

A_1 13.67
B 1.45
A_2 4.33

Figure 16 shows his record for the seatwork periods.

EVALUATION

The objective was accomplished. The child enjoyed seeing himself do well.

Implications for the use of behavior modification materials: Graphs.

Other materials that might have been useful: Contract forms, tokens, menu, and high-interest activities.

CLASS: Second Grade
BEHAVIOR: Talking Out, Touching Others, and Incorrect Posture

CIRCUMSTANCES
A second-grade class of twenty-seven students had fifteen students above average and four below average.

TARGET BEHAVIOR
During daily group lessons in which the children were seated on the floor, the following behaviors were counted:

1. Talking out while someone else is talking or reading
2. Touching another child, especially playing with hair or leaning on another
3. Posture in any position other than sitting on the floor

BEHAVIORAL OBJECTIVE
To reduce target behaviors to a point where they no longer interfere with the teaching process.

EXPERIMENTAL DESIGN

A_1	2 days
B	9 days
A_2	1 week

INTERVENTION
For every lesson the children completed with five or less bad manners, they received a sticker portraying an Indian which was attached to a chart. A lesson with no bad manners resulted in two Indian stickers. A mark was put on the chalkboard whenever a bad manner was observed. If the children earned nine stickers in nine days, they received Good Work Awards that they could take home.

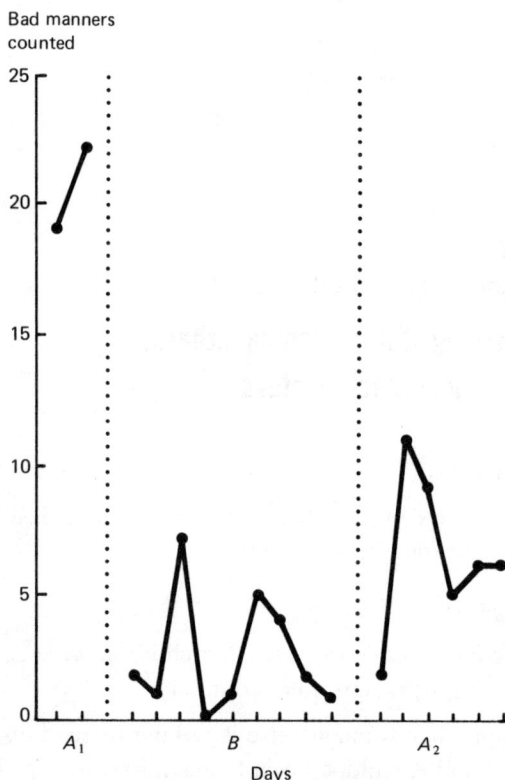

FIGURE 17. Number of bad manners counted while seated on the floor for group lessons, A_1 to A_2.

RESULTS

The mean number of bad manners counted per day while seated on the floor is shown in Figure 17 and can be summarized as follows.

	Mean
A_1	20.5
B	2.7
A_2	7.4

EVALUATION

The objective was accomplished. When intervention was removed for the reversal, the children's behavior remained far better than before intervention.

Implications for use of materials: Graphing, sticker tokens, awards for good work.

Note: The nine-day deadline could have led to frustration if the children had not done so well. The reward after nine stickers, no deadline, might be a generally better intervention.

CLASS: Second and Third Grade Transitional
BEHAVIOR: Raising Hand to Verbalize During Reading

CIRCUMSTANCES

The reading group consisted of nine children, two girls and seven boys. The children generally failed to raise hands to answer questions. The teacher had difficulty ascertaining which children knew answers and which did not. Some children seemed to merely echo an answer shouted out by another child.

TARGET BEHAVIOR

Children did not raise hands to answer questions. *Hand raising* is defined as a movement of the hand upward so that the hand, from tip of fingers to wrist, was six inches above the shoulder.

BEHAVIORAL OBJECTIVE

To increase the number of times that hands are raised to answer questions asked by the teacher.

EXPERIMENTAL DESIGN

A_1	10 days
B	13 days
A_2	8 days

INTERVENTION

The teacher followed each daily reading lesson with eighteen comprehension questions, so that each of the nine children would have the chance to answer two questions per day.

The program involved the use of graphing, with free time as a back-up reinforcer. A chart was posted in the reading corner. It contained the children's names with space after each for the accumulation of points awarded for hand-raising behavior. The points were recorded as stars, and every five stars were worth 15 minutes of free time. The stars were exchanged for minutes of free time on Friday afternoon. Each child could earn two stars per day or ten each week, which meant that the most free time a child could earn was 30 minutes a week and there was ample opportunity to earn at least 15 minutes.

RESULTS

The number of questions answered with a hand raise are shown in the following table and in Figure 18.

	Mean	Median
A_1	4.8	5
B	14.4	16
A_2	12.7	13

EVALUATION

The objective was accomplished and a reinstatement of the program was planned. The teacher observed an increase in class enthusiasm as a result of the program, and she also felt that the group was achieving more academically.

Implications for use of behavior modification materials: Graphing, token materials, back-up reinforcers, and high-interest materials.

Other materials that might have been used: Contract forms.

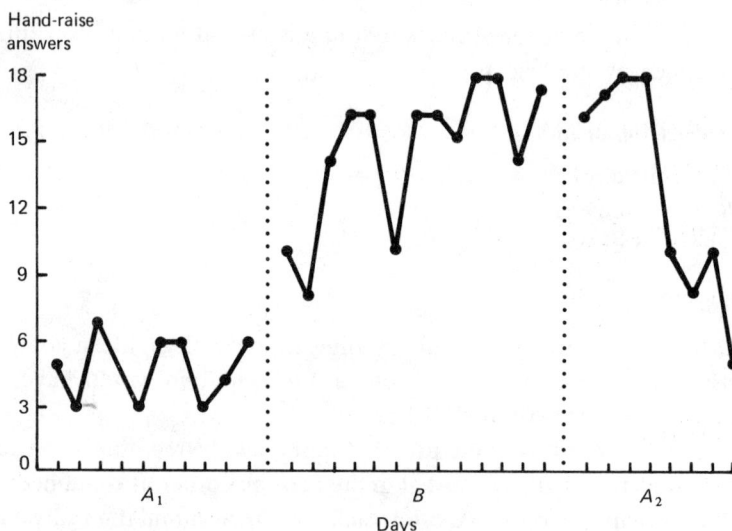

FIGURE 18. Number of questions answered with a raised hand per day, A_1 to A_2.

CLASS: Second and Third Grade Transitional
BEHAVIOR: Coming Up for Reading Group after First Call

CIRCUMSTANCES

Five nine-year-old children were in the same reading group in a class of twenty-four students. Two of the five children in the reading group were considered disruptive by the teacher, and might dawdle in coming to the reading group in order to see the teacher become irritated. All five of the children were very slow in coming to the front of the room for reading. This resulted in each child having less time to read and/or less time to do the reading assignments.

TARGET BEHAVIOR

The teacher counted the number of seconds it took each child to join the group with his reader and workbook.

BEHAVIORAL OBJECTIVE

To reduce the amount of time needed for the children to form a group in the reading area to approximately 30 seconds.

EXPERIMENTAL DESIGN

A_1	5 days
B	10 days
A_2	5 days

INTERVENTION

Those children who came to the reading group within 30 seconds after the first call were allowed to go to lunch two minutes early. The teacher openly recorded the amount of time it took the students to arrive during intervention and kept a graph of the times.

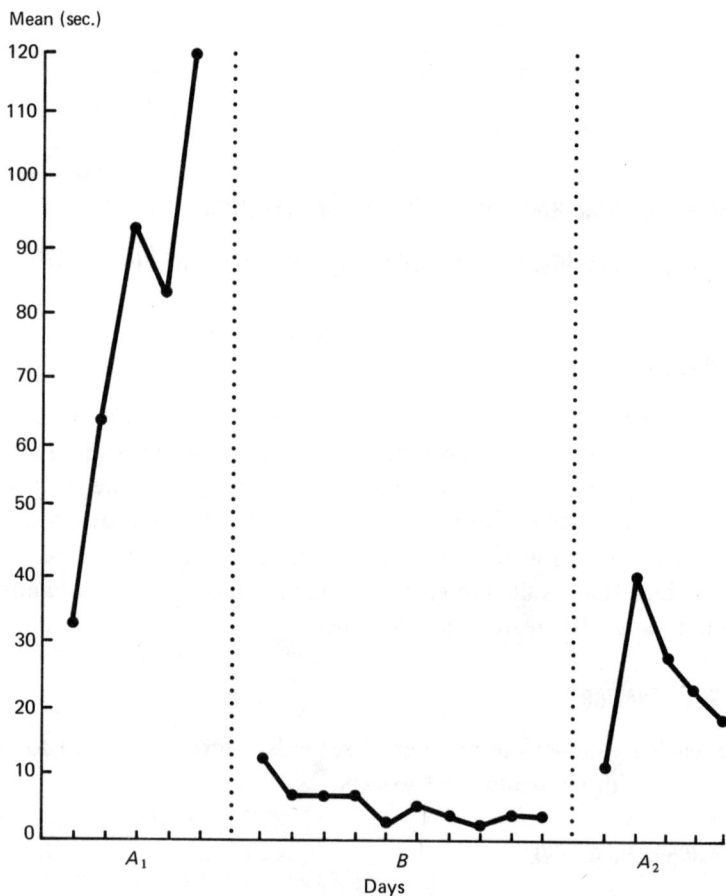

FIGURE 19.   Mean number of seconds for the five children to come to their reading group, A_1 to A_2.

RESULTS

The number of seconds per day between first call for reading and arrival of each student in the reading group is shown in Figure 19.

	Mean	Median
A_1	79.2 sec.	35 sec.
B	6.0	3.0
A_2	22.4	20.0

EVALUATION

Intervention was extremely successful, and the children far surpassed the objective. In addition, they seemed more interested and attentive. The effects of the program seemed to spread to other reading groups. The extremely short times of arrival in the group during intervention were possible because the children came to anticipate the teacher's directions and would often take appropriate places even before called. **Implications** for use of materials: Timers, graphs, back-up reinforcer.

CLASS: Third Grade
BEHAVIOR: Neat Worksheets

CIRCUMSTANCE

The classroom contained twenty third-grade students. There were no known physical or mental handicaps among them. The mean age was approximately eight years old.

TARGET BEHAVIOR

To decrease the number of reading worksheets that were not completed neatly. *Neatness* is defined as (1) printing between lines, not under or over lines; (2) words separated by a space; (3) clean erasures, no dark smudges; (4) no crumpled or torn papers.

BEHAVIOR OBJECTIVE

To significantly increase the number of worksheets that meet the neatness criteria in a fourteen-day period.

EXPERIMENTAL DESIGN

A_1 3 days
B 14 days
A_2 5 days

INTERVENTION

Originally, when a child turned in messy papers, he might receive a lecture or be told to redo the papers. Usually, nothing happened.

Intervention utilized a bulletin board entitled "Turkey Shooting for Neatness." It was November. A drawing of a large turkey and twenty rifles was on the board. Each rifle was labeled with a child's name and the "bullets" were color-coded tokens. Whenever a child completed two neat reading papers, he earned a "bang," and the word was printed on the papers. The child then received a bullet placed after his rifle on the bulletin board. Students who "hit" the turkey by November 28 received a Good Work certificate of achievement with a red velvet ribbon attached. Students who did not hit the turkey, but who improved, received the reward without the ribbon. The certificates read "Good Work Award: for neatness on reading papers, to _____" and signed by the teacher. The paper was a bright color with a fancy diploma-like border.

RESULTS

The following figures represent the number of students who turned in at least two neat papers per day.

	Mean
A_1	3.6
B	13.2
A_2	12.2

Figure 20 shows the number of students with neat worksheets for each day from baseline to reversal.

EVALUATION

Intervention was definitely successful. However, checking papers was time consuming. The primary ability of each child was taken into consideration and objectivity was sometimes difficult.

Implications for the use of behavior modification materials: Graphing, tokens, certificates of achievement.

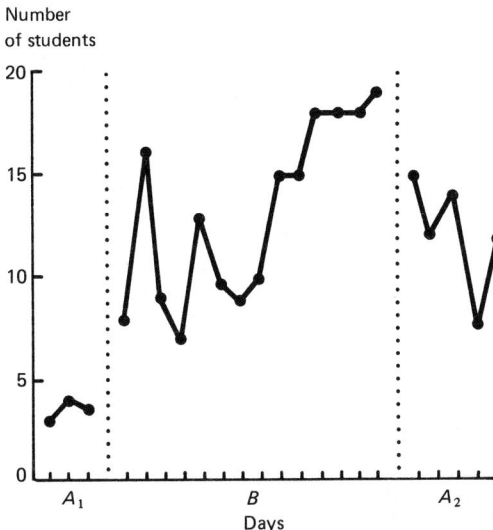

FIGURE 20.   Number of students completing at least two neat reading papers, A_1 to A_2.

CLASS: Third Grade
BEHAVIOR: Studying

CIRCUMSTANCES

The child in question might be labeled borderline or mildly retarded. She was reading on a beginning preprimer level with difficulty. Previous teachers had described the child as aggressive, nonconforming, and attention seeking. The child exhibited many behaviors incompatible with studying and learning such as noise making, incessant talking, failure to attend to directions, and being out of seat.

TARGET BEHAVIOR

Child's behaviors that were incompatible with studying and learning. *Studying* was defined as being in seat, attempting work, paper on desk in front of pupil, and pencil or crayon in hand.

BEHAVIORAL OBJECTIVE

To increase the amount of the student's on-task behavior—being in her seat, attempting work, paper in front of her, and pencil or crayon in hand for a 20-minute period each morning.

EXPERIMENTAL DESIGN

A_1 18 days
B 19 days
A_2 10 days

INTERVENTION

The program called for the use of graphing and the use of free time as a back-up reinforcer. A paraprofessional kept a record on a grid, and a square was checked every 30 seconds. If the child was studying during the 30 seconds, a "+" was recorded. If not, a "−" was recorded.

A second chart was kept by the child. If she was studying, she was told to make stars after 1- to 5-minute intervals. A row of stars was exchangeable for 5 minutes of free time with the paraprofessional. During the first week of intervention, there were six stars in a row. After the first week, each row had room for eight stars.

Two separate records were ideal. The chart made by the child provided visual incentive for her. The record kept by the paraprofessional provided precise data and avoided confusion when the child periodically destroyed her chart. (The chart destruction occurred when the child gave herself unearned stars and was reprimanded by the teacher.)

RESULTS

The percentages of time spent on task (studying) during a 20-minute period from baseline through reversal are shown in Figure 21 and in the following table.

	Mean	Median
A_1	13.1%	6%
B	66.6	70
A_2	32.3	28.5

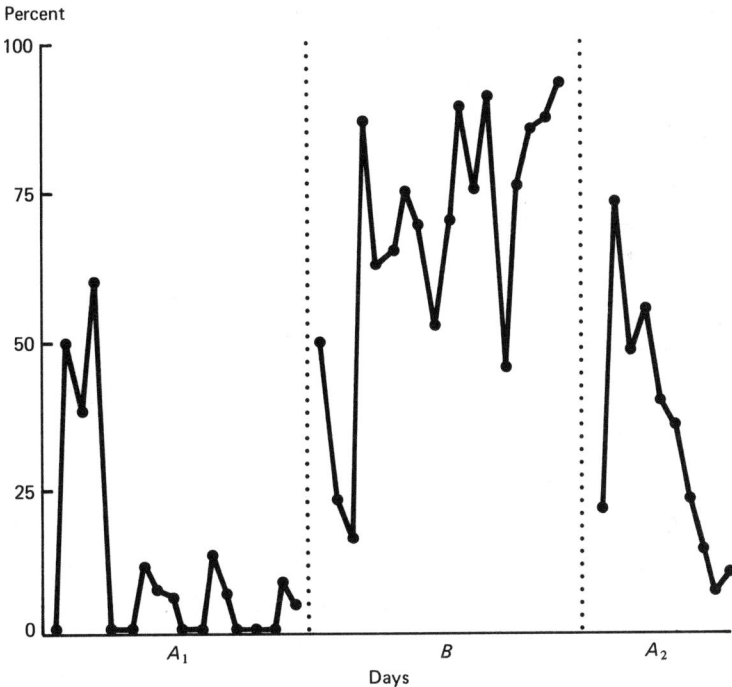

FIGURE 21.   Percent of 20-minute periods the child spent studying, A_1 to A_2.

The teacher suggested that the three good days during baseline (see Figure 21) were very atypical. The child apparently became aware of the data collection procedure being carried out by the paraprofessional.

EVALUATION

The objective was accomplished so well that the teacher reinstated the program, but without the precise data collecting. She described the effects of the program as "heavenly."

Implications for use of materials: Graphing forms, token materials, timers, back-up reinforcers, and high-interest materials.

Other materials that might have been used: Menus and contract forms.

CLASS: Fourth Grade, Reading Group
BEHAVIOR: Talking Out

CIRCUMSTANCES

Four boys in a reading group frequently talked out during reading lessons. All were ten years old. Two of the boys had long histories of disturbing classrooms.

TARGET BEHAVIOR

Talking out, meaning any audible verbalization not solicited by the teacher. Appropriate talking was when the teacher directed the student to talk, as in calling on him to recite, or when she recognized the student's raised hand.

BEHAVIORAL OBJECTIVE

To decrease talking out to a point where the behavior no longer interfered with the lesson and preferably to eliminate the behavior.

EXPERIMENTAL DESIGN

A_1 5 days
B 10 days
A_2 5 days

INTERVENTION

Before intervention, talking out behavior was verbally reprimanded by the teacher. During intervention, a kitchen timer was set to go off seven times during the 30-minute reading period. The reading group was told that a point would be awarded to them whenever there was no on-going inappropriate behavior when the timer went off. A total of five points at the end of the class period earned the use of a basketball for the recess which followed the reading class. One class member could ruin the score. At the ringing of the timer, the teacher either marked a point on the board if there was no talking out, or remained seated if there was talking out. The children could not see the timer-face to know when it would ring.

RESULTS

The number of times the four boys talked out during 30-minute reading lessons is shown in Figure 22 and in the following table.

	Mean	Median
A_1	35.2	36
B	13.9	11
A_2	19.8	16

EVALUATION

The objective was met, but not to the degree desired. A longer intervention period as well as some variety in the rewards made available would probably have yielded more satisfactory results.

Implications for use of materials: Timers, graphs, high-interest activities.

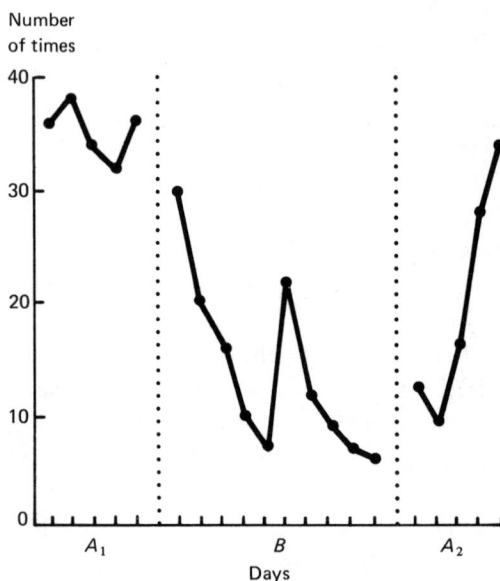

FIGURE 22. Number of times four boys talked out during 30-minute reading classes, A_1 to A_2.

CLASS: Fourth Grade
BEHAVIOR: Writing Multiplication Facts from Memory

CIRCUMSTANCES

The students were the thirty-three members of a fourth-grade class. There was a need for the children to have immediate recall of the multiplication facts from 0 through 10 in order to progress through their fourth-grade math work. Previously, the children used "facts" charts, but there were few who seemed to be making any concentrated effort to memorize the multiplication charts.

During baseline and intervention, a daily multiplication facts quiz was given. The quiz consisted of twenty items presented orally the first thing each morning to which the students simply wrote the products. An A was a "perfect" paper, that is, all twenty items correct.

TARGET BEHAVIOR

Few students had immediate recall of multiplication facts. The teacher counted the number of students who received A's on the multiplication quiz, assuming that this number would be a measure of multiplication achievement.

BEHAVIORAL OBJECTIVE

To increase the percentage of the class earning A's on the daily multiplication facts quiz.

EXPERIMENTAL DESIGN

A_1 8 days
B 30 days
A_2 9 days

INTERVENTION

During baseline, the children simply took the quizzes. The intervention program involved the use of graphing. Two large charts were

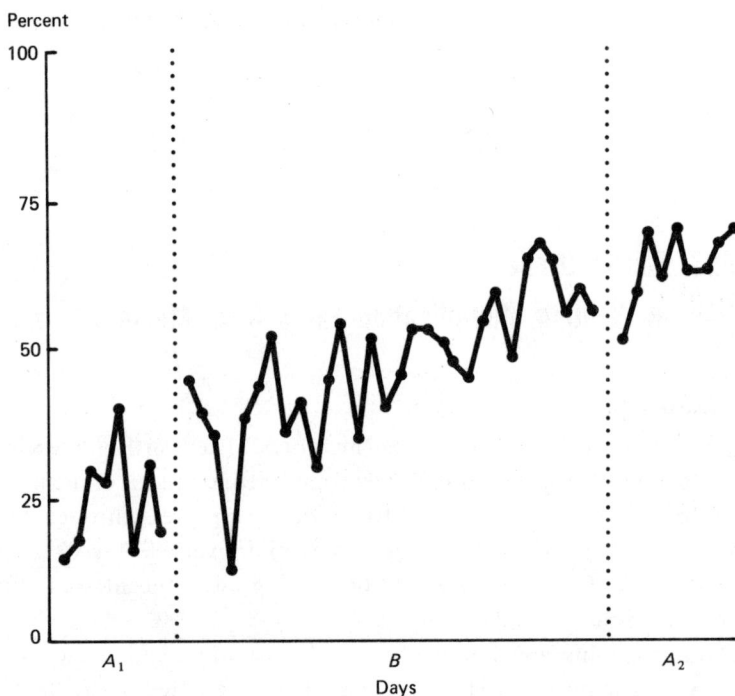

FIGURE 23. Percentage of class earning A's on daily multiplication facts quiz, A_1 to A_2.

posted on the bulletin board. One listed each student's name and showed a star for each time the student received an A on the facts quiz. The other chart showed team performance, boys against the girls. At the end of the week, A's for each team were totaled and the winning team received a treat.

After the third week of intervention, the teacher felt that the same people were earning A's for their team, so the reward was changed from a group basis to an individual basis. On the sixteenth day of the program, only those who had earned three A's during the week received a treat, regardless of team. The winning team earned an unscheduled recess.

Each student also kept his own personal chart on which he recorded his own success rate each day.

RESULTS

The percentage of students completing perfect quizzes (A's) per day is shown in Figure 23 and summarized in the following table.

	Mean	Median
A_1	24%	24%
B	50	48
A_2	62	63

EVALUATION

The objective was met. All students increased their mastery of multiplication facts, and many of the students earned A's consistently. Through the team approach, the students developed a group spirit so as to increase both cooperation and competition. Self-recorded charts were most helpful in developing personal responsibility.

Implications for use of behavior modification materials: Graphing forms (group and individual), token materials, back-up reinforcers, and high-interest materials.

CLASS: Fourth Grade
BEHAVIOR: Being Prompt Coming in from Recess

CIRCUMSTANCES

The thirty-one children in the fourth-grade self-contained classroom were very slow coming back to class after recess. Many minutes of class time were wasted daily. The original consequence for being late was a verbal reprimand from the teacher.

TARGET BEHAVIOR

Slow return to class from recess, with loss of class time; the teacher kept a record of the number of students in-seat and with coats off 3 minutes after the recess bell rang.

BEHAVIORAL OBJECTIVE

For the children to return to class, take off coats, and be seated within 3 minutes of the end of recess. (End of recess was signaled by a bell or by the teacher.)

EXPERIMENTAL DESIGN

A_1	10 days
B_1	20 days
A_2	5 days
B_2	9 days

The teacher continued to count the behavior for nine days during reinstatement (B_2), when she introduced intervention for the second time.

INTERVENTION

The children were told that if 95 percent of the children present that day at school were at their desks within the allotted amount of time, they

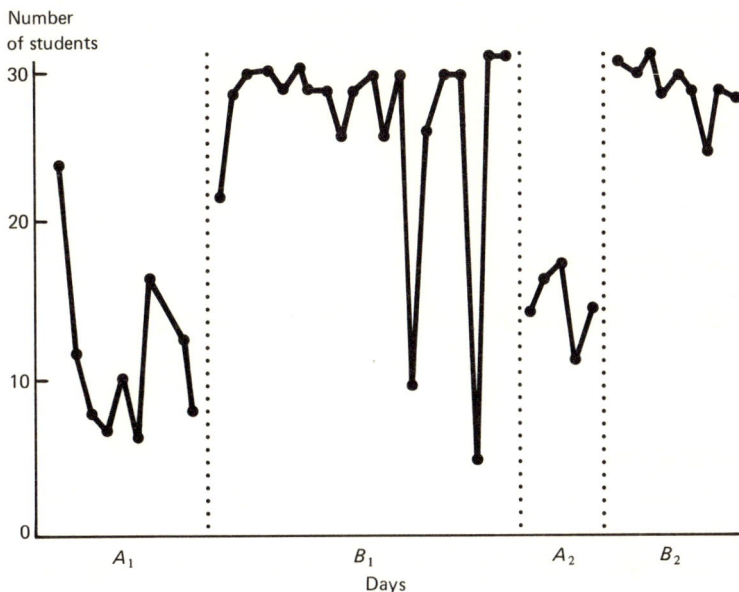

FIGURE 24. Number of students seated at desks within 3 minutes of the end
of recess, baseline (A_1) through reinstatement (B_2).

would receive an extra minute of recess. The extra time would be added
to the Friday morning recess period.

RESULTS

Out of the thirty-one children, the number that were prompt returning
from recess is shown in Figure 24 and the following table.

	Mean	Median
A_1	12.0	11.5
B_1	27.3	29
A_2	18.7	15
B_2	29.3	30

EVALUATION

The first intervention period was very successful in meeting the objective, and the children did poorly on only two days. On those days, the
school bells were out of order. During B_1, the children met the 95 percent criterion on all days except the first, fourteenth, fifteenth, and
eighteenth days; in B_2 the criterion was met on all but the seventh day.
Implications for use of materials: Record sheets, timers, back-up reinforcers.

CLASS: EMR, Intermediate
BEHAVIOR: Mastery of Basic Addition Facts

CIRCUMSTANCES

The subject for this study is an eleven-year-old boy enrolled in an intermediate class for educable mentally retarded children.

TARGET BEHAVIOR

The boy's rote mastery of the thirty-six basic addition facts was considered below his capability level.

BEHAVIORAL OBJECTIVE

To increase the number of addition facts known by rote when presented with flash card stimuli for 3 seconds during a work period each morning.

EXPERIMENTAL DESIGN

A_1 10 days
B 12 days
A_2 10 days

INTERVENTION

During baseline and reversal periods, no token reinforcement was given for appropriate on-task behavior.

The program involved the use of tokens and premiums as back-up reinforcers. Each time a correct response was given, it was reinforced with a token coupled with praise. The tokens were exchangeable at the rate of three tokens for one cent. Money earned could be used to purchase items of food from the cafeteria, a model, a record, or a toy car.

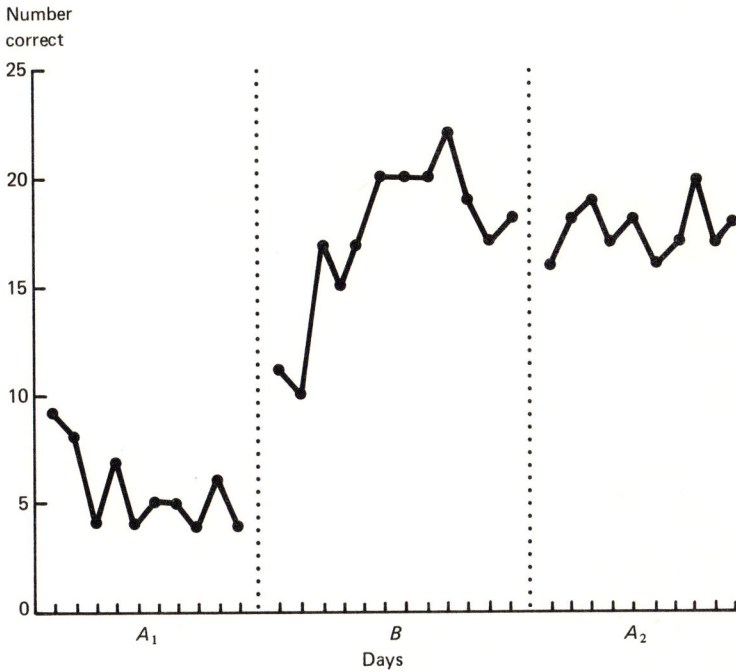

FIGURE 25.   Number of addition facts known (out of 36) by an eleven-year-old EMR child, A_1 to A_2.

RESULTS

The number of addition facts the boy knew when presented with flash cards, each shown for 3 seconds, is shown in Figure 25 and the following table.

	Mean	Median
A_1	5.6	5.0
B	17.2	17.5
A_2	17.6	17.5

EVALUATION

The objective was accomplished—the boy's rote mastery of basic addition facts from baseline to reversal more than tripled.

Implications for the use of behavior modification materials: Token materials, premiums, and menu forms.

CLASS: Fourth and Fifth Grade, Hearing Impaired
BEHAVIOR: Time Taken to Change Class Activities

CIRCUMSTANCES

The subjects for this study were eight fourth- and fifth-grade students, ages eleven to twelve, in a class for the hearing impaired.

TARGET BEHAVIOR

Students were taking more time than was desired by the teacher to change from one class activity to another.

BEHAVIORAL OBJECTIVE

To decrease the time the students took to respond to the teacher's announcement of a new activity, "Now it's time to _____" (scheduled activity). *Respond* means the students are at their desks, quiet, and ready to work.

EXPERIMENTAL DESIGN

A_1 6 days
B 12 days
A_2 5 days

INTERVENTION

During baseline and reversal periods, no token reinforcement was given for appropriate on-task behavior.

The program involved the use of tokens with privileges as back-up reinforcers. The first student ready to work after the teacher's statement (see objective) was given eight tokens, the second received seven, and so on. When the student earned a specified number of tokens, he could "buy" a pass to physical education class. This class was made up of sixth graders, had a male teacher, and was very much prized by all the students in the study.

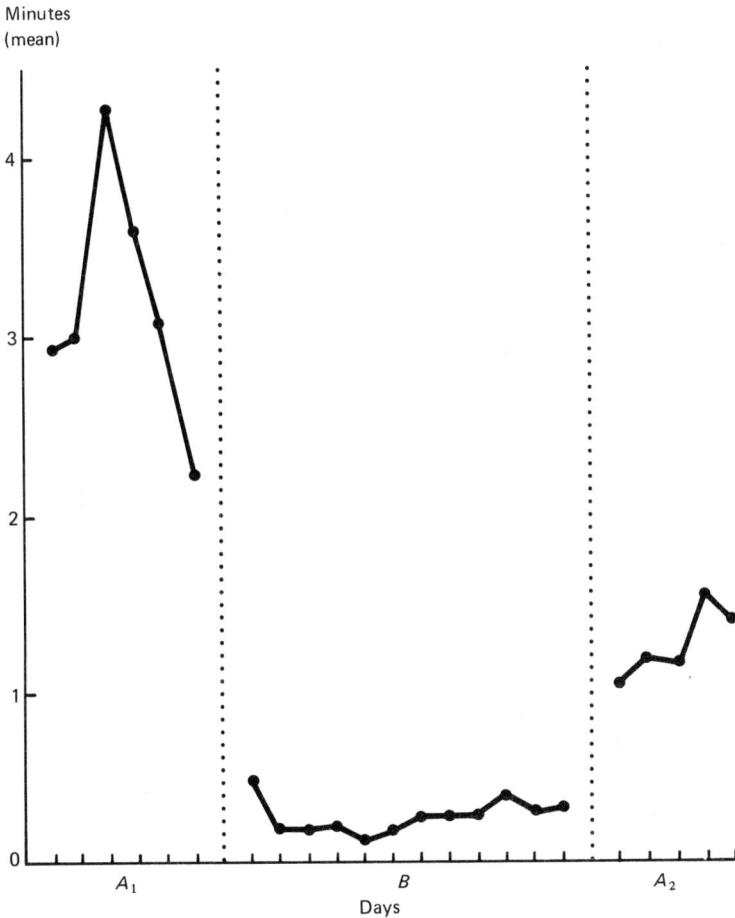

FIGURE 26. Mean number of minutes used per day by eight students to change activities, A_1 to A_2.

RESULTS

The number of minutes taken to change activities (four changes per day) was counted and averaged per day, as shown in Figure 26 and the following table.

	Mean	Median
A_1	3 min. 11 sec.	3 min. 3 sec.
B	18 sec.	18 sec.
A_2	1 min. 16 sec.	1 min. 11 sec.

EVALUATION

The objective was accomplished. The teacher was also aware of the development of good sportsmanship, fair play, and honesty during the project.

Implications for the use of behavior modification materials: Token materials, premiums, timers.

CLASS: Special Intermediate
BEHAVIOR: Completion of Math Assignments

CIRCUMSTANCES

The subject in this study was a thirteen-year-old boy who was a member of a nongraded, highly individualized center. He was moderately retarded, emotionally disturbed, and had been in residential care prior to placement at the center.

TARGET BEHAVIOR

Completion of math assignments was considered below capability level. (*Completion* was the number of math problems the boy completed correctly, as counted by the teacher.)

BEHAVIORAL OBJECTIVE

To increase the number of two-place subtraction problems with borrowing that were correctly completed during a 15-minute period each day.

EXPERIMENTAL DESIGN

A_1 10 days
B 23 days
A_2 10 days

INTERVENTION

During baseline and reversal periods no token reinforcement was used for appropriate on-task behavior.

The program involved the use of token reinforcement. One token was awarded each time 20 problems in the specified area were completed within the specified 15 minutes. Another token was given each time more math problems were completed than those completed the previous day. Fifteen tokens merited a model car.

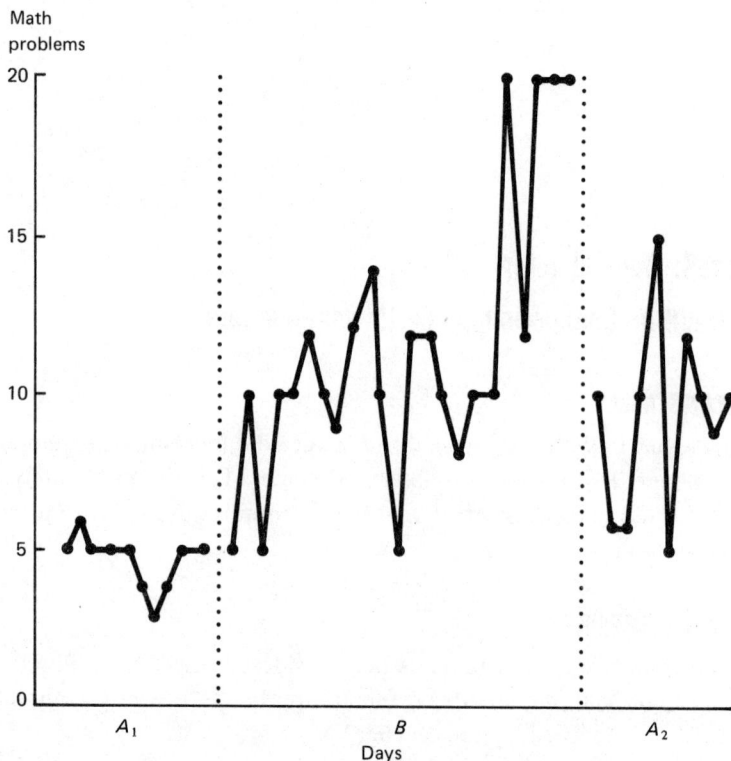

FIGURE 27.   Number of math problems completed in 15 minutes by a moderately retarded thirteen-year-old boy, A_1 to A_2.

RESULTS

The number of math problems completed in a 15-minute period was counted, as shown in Figure 27 and the following table.

	Mean	Median
A_1	4.7	5
B	11.6	10
A_2	9.3	10

EVALUATION

The objective was accomplished. The number of math problems completed increased at a gradual rate until the student accomplished the goal of 20 problems within a 15-minute period during intervention. **Implications** for the use of behavior modification materials: Token materials and premiums.

CLASS: Fifth Grade
BEHAVIOR: Naming Synonyms

CIRCUMSTANCES
The subject for this study was an eleven-year-old boy with a learning disability participating in a regular fifth-grade class with difficulty.

TARGET BEHAVIOR
The boy's use of correct synonyms in oral language was considered below his capability level.

BEHAVIORAL OBJECTIVE
To achieve 90 percent accuracy in supplying synonyms for 20 words on a mimeographed page during a daily 7-minute period. Different words appeared on the list each day.

EXPERIMENTAL DESIGN
A_1	4 days
B	4 days
A_2	4 days

INTERVENTION
During baseline and reversal periods, no token reinforcement was given for appropriate on-task behavior.

The program involved the use of positive reinforcement in the form of social praise, token reinforcement in the form of points, and the privilege of play as the back-up reinforcer. Initially, verbal praise was given for every correct response. As accuracy improved, verbal praise was lowered to every fifth response. At the same time, one point was awarded for every two correct responses. Each point counted toward 1 minute of playing time in the game area at the end of the session.

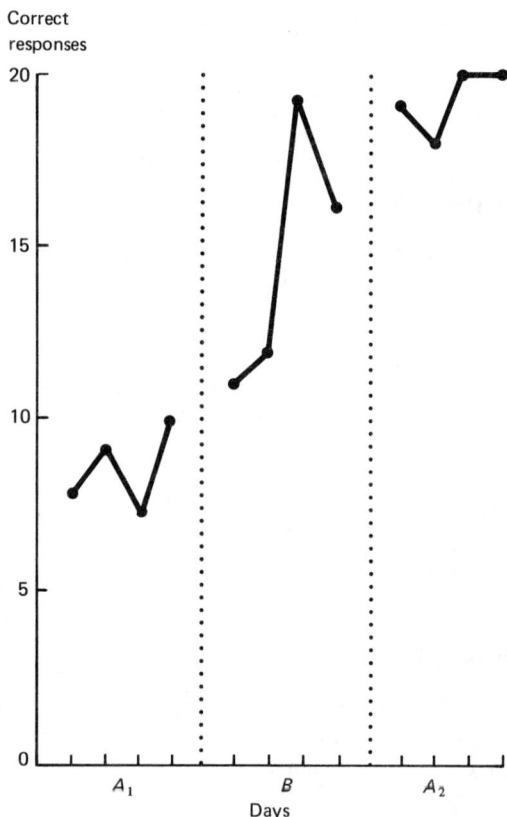

FIGURE 28. Number of correct synonyms supplied for 20-word lists in a daily 7-minute period, A_1 to A_2.

RESULTS

The number of correct synonyms supplied to the 20-word lists was counted each day, as shown in Figure 28 and the following table.

	Mean	Median
A_1	9.0	8.0
B	17.0	15.0
A_2	19.0	19.5

EVALUATION

The objective of 90 percent accuracy was achieved when the child's score reached 18 or more, and this was accomplished during intervention and reversal. The boy's attitude as well as his performance improved.

Implications for the use of behavior modification materials: Rewards (praise), token materials, and back-up reinforcers.

Other materials that might have been used: graphing, contract forms.

CLASS: Eighth Grade, Deaf
BEHAVIOR: Speaking Out

CIRCUMSTANCES

The subjects for this project were three deaf students enrolled in a regular eighth grade but receiving tutorial help.

TARGET BEHAVIOR

During class discussions, subjects spoke out regardless of whether or not it was their turn.

BEHAVIORAL OBJECTIVE

To decrease the number of interruptions made by the deaf students shouting out in a 50-minute class period each day.

EXPERIMENTAL DESIGN

A_1 9 days
B 8 days
A_2 5 days

INTERVENTION

The program involved the use of positive reinforcement in the form of teacher's smiles and/or words of approval. The students were asked to look and see if someone else was speaking before they proceeded to speak. Every time they did so, they were positively reinforced by the teacher.

RESULTS

The number of interruptions by the deaf students in a daily 50-minute period was counted, as shown in Figure 29 and the following table.

	Mean	Median
A_1	14.55	15.0
B	4.0	4.0
A_2	6.00	6.0

EVALUATION

The objective of decreasing interruptions was accomplished. The teacher felt, however, that the students also decreased in enthusiasm and spontaneity. Therefore, the program was not reinstated and interruptions still did not return to baseline level.

Implications for the use of behavior modification materials: Rewards.

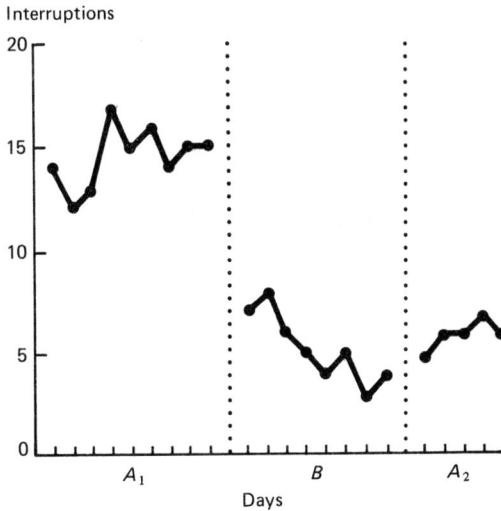

FIGURE 29.   Number of interruptions by three deaf students in a daily 50-minute period, A_1 to A_2.

CLASS: Junior High, Hard of Hearing
BEHAVIOR: Accurate Spelling on Spelling Tests

CIRCUMSTANCES

Four hard-of-hearing students attended regular junior high classes, but they often had difficulty with language. Pronunciation, spelling, and the use of service words that connect concrete nouns were especially difficult for these children. The teacher presented 20 service words from the Dolch list (a basic primary vocabulary list of 220 words) to the hard-of-hearing students twice a week. The students were also tested for spelling accuracy of the 20 words twice each week.

TARGET BEHAVIOR

The behavior counted for each student was the number of correctly spelled words written when given a spelling test of 20 words.

BEHAVIORAL OBJECTIVE

To increase the number of correctly spelled words enough to achieve 90 percent (18 words out of 20 correct) accuracy on spelling tests.

EXPERIMENTAL DESIGN

A_1 3 tests
B_1 3 tests
A_2 3 tests
B_2 2 tests

INTERVENTION

The intervention programs involved the use of thermometer-type graphing. The graphs were made of cardboard with spaces that the children could color. One space was colored for each correct answer on a spelling test. No back-up reinforcer was used.

During baseline (A_1) and reversal (A_2) periods, no graphing was used.

Words correct
(mean number)

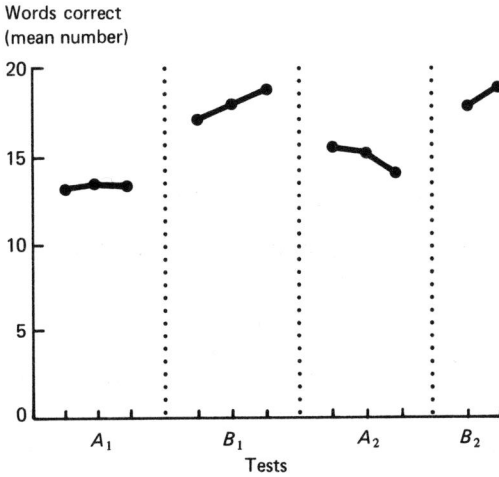

FIGURE 30.   Mean number of correctly spelled words per test for four hard-of-hearing students, from baseline (A_1) to reinstatement (B_2).

RESULTS

The average number of words spelled correctly per test is shown in Figure 30 and in the following table.

	Mean	Median
A_1	13.3	13.5
B_1	17.8	18.0
A_2	15.0	15.5
B_2	18.2	18.5

EVALUATION

The intervention program accomplished the objectives in 9 of 12 test papers during B_1 and in 6 of 8 test papers during B_2. The mean score in B_2 surpassed the objective of 90 percent accuracy. The teacher felt that the intervention provided the assurance that the students needed regarding success in school. Since all students improved during intervention, the teacher now uses the graphs regularly.

Implications for the use of behavior modification materials: Graphing.
Other materials that might have been used: Contract forms, token materials, certificates of achievement.

CLASS: Ninth Grade
BEHAVIOR: Bringing Materials to Class

CIRCUMSTANCES

A secondary school area studies class of twenty-seven students met daily. Reading and written assignments were geared for "average" students. To do the assignments, each student needed to bring to class each day (1) a notebook, (2) pen or pencil, (3) syllabus, and (4) textbook.

TARGET BEHAVIOR

Many students did not bring the necessary materials to class. Without them, they could not perform the assignments to meet course requirements.

BEHAVIORAL OBJECTIVE

To increase the rate of bringing materials to class so that materials were present every day.

EXPERIMENTAL DESIGN

A_1 10 days
B 10 days
A_2 9 days

INTERVENTION

During baseline, the students were already earning points for homework, notebook work, tests, and so forth, and the points were used in determining grades. The intervention program called for giving extra points for bringing each of the four materials. Bringing all of the materials earned the student a total of four points; for each missing article one point was subtracted from this total. At the end of the grading period, the student's total point accumulation was considered in giving the student a "special" grade for bringing materials.

The student saw the point value he had earned daily on the teacher's record sheets. It was hoped that the student would come to be rewarded by having what he needed to do his work and that the behavior would not deteriorate during reversal.

RESULTS

The average number of 4 needed materials brought to class per day by the twenty-seven students was counted, as shown in Figure 31. The results from baseline through reversal were as follows:

	Mean
A_1	1.1
B	3.4
A_2	2.9

EVALUATION

The objective was met on five of the ten intervention days. The teacher indicated that the improvement (over 200 percent) was more than he had expected.

Implications for use of materials: Record sheets and tokens.

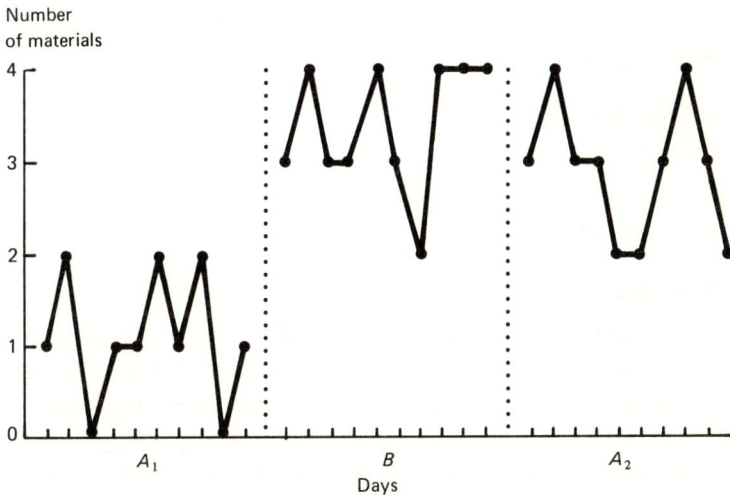

FIGURE 31. Mean number of materials (of four needed) brought to class, A_1 to A_2.

CLASS: Senior High, Driver Education
BEHAVIOR: Answering without Raising Hand

CIRCUMSTANCES

The subject in this study was a high-school boy in a driver education class of thirty students. He appeared to have average intelligence but did not apply himself.

TARGET BEHAVIOR

Subject shouted out in class, giving incorrect or irrelevant answers. The teacher counted the times the student verbalized an answer without raising his hand.

BEHAVIORAL OBJECTIVE

To decrease the number of times in a daily two-hour class session the student shouted out answers without raising his hand and waiting for the teacher to respond, in an eight-day period.

EXPERIMENTAL DESIGN

A_1 4 days
B 8 days
A_2 4 days

INTERVENTION

During baseline and reversal periods, the teacher acknowledged all answers, appropriate or inappropriate, as politely as possible.

The program involved the use of a contract involving grades. The contract stated that the grades on weekly quizzes would be upgraded one level if shouting out behavior was reduced (D raised to C, C to B, and B to A). If the student wanted to respond, he was to raise his hand and wait for the teacher's acknowledgment. At least 50 percent of the student's answers had to be correct.

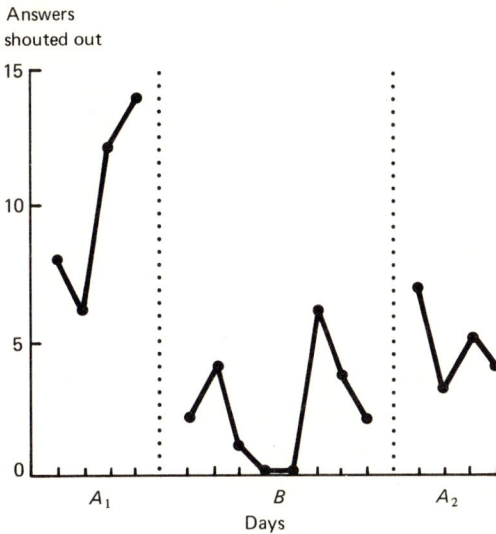

FIGURE 32.   Number of answers a student shouted out per class, A_1 to A_2.

RESULTS

The number of answers the student shouted out per class was counted, as shown in Figure 32 and the following table.

	Mean	Median
A_1	10.0	10.0
B	2.37	2.0
A_2	4.75	4.5

EVALUATION

The objective was accomplished. Unwanted behavior decreased and academic achievement increased as a result of this project. No substantial increase in shouting out behavior occurred after the intervention program was stopped.

Implications for the use of behavior modification materials: Contract forms and token materials.

Answers to Review Questions
Chapters 1 through 10

CHAPTER 1
1. behavior
2. quantify
3. waste
4. D
5. observations of behavior
6. how frequently a behavior will occur

CHAPTER 2
1. antecedents . . . consequences
2. time
3. cues
4. consequences
5. gain something . . . get away from something
6. positive reinforcement
7. negative reinforcement
8. increase in frequency
9. decrease in frequency

CHAPTER 3
1. a consequence that causes the behavior preceding the consequence to increase
2. counting the behavior

CHAPTER 4
1. humane, sociological, "punishment" may be a

(Chapter 4, cont.)
   reward, basic operant principles, respondent conditioning
2. rewards . . . punishments

CHAPTER 5
1. generalization
2. discrimination
3. generalization . . . discrimination
4. generalize
5. discriminate

CHAPTER 6
1. shaping . . . fading
2. fading . . . faded
3. Shaping . . . reinforced
4. extinction

CHAPTER 7
1. no shaping or fading are required
2. (a) knowing which behaviors you do and do not want
   (b) which of these compliment each other
   (c) what contingencies are available

(Chapter 7, cont.)

3. (a) the behavior is dangerous to people or jeopardizes equipment
   (b) the behavior is self-reinforcing
4. (a) behavior you will begin with
   (b) you plan to count the behavior
   (c) collect baseline data
   (d) the contingency program will be
   (e) you will eliminate at least part of the program

CHAPTER 8

1. shaping . . . fading
2. beginning . . . end
3. Pavlovian
4. smart

CHAPTER 9

1. a symbol exchangeable for a reinforcer
2. math, banking, economics etc.
3. reinforced inappropriate behaviors

(Chapter 9, cont.)

4. (a) individualization of reinforcement
   (b) expansion of reinforcing alternatives
   (c) added structure and/or unstructured time to class routine
   (d) facilitation of immediate reinforcement
   (e) added variety and excitement to the class

CHAPTER 10

1. fixed interval, variable interval, fixed ratio, variable ratio
2. frequency of the response; the passage of time
3. *fixed interval*
   —scalloped effect
   variable interval
   —slow, consistent
   fixed ratio
   —stepped, all or nonresponding
   variable ratio
   —fast, consistent

Index

DATE DUE